THE UNQUIET GRAVE

THE
UNQUIET
GRAVE

A WORD CYCLE

BY

PALINURUS

REVISED EDITION
WITH AN INTRODUCTION BY
CYRIL CONNOLLY

PERSEA BOOKS   NEW YORK

The publisher wishes to acknowledge Burt Britton for his
help in making this edition of THE UNQUIET GRAVE
possible.

Copyright © 1981 by Deirdre Levi.

For information, contact the publisher:

Persea Books
225 Lafayette St.
New York, N.Y. 10012

All Rights Reserved.

ISBN 0-89255-058-9
Library of Congress Catalog Card Number 81-82929
First published in *Horizon* 1944
First Persea Edition, 1981
Second Persea Edition, 1982
Printed in the United States of America

CONTENTS

'Palinurus, a skilful pilot of the ship of Æneas fell into the sea in his sleep, was three days exposed to the tempests and waves of the sea and at last came safe to the seashore near Velia, where the cruel inhabitants of the place murdered him to obtain his clothes: his body was left unburied on the seashore.'

LEMPRIÈRE

'Mox vero Lucanis pestilentia laborantibus respondit oraculum, Manes Palinuri esse placandos: ob quam rem non longe a Velia et lucum et cenotaphium ei dederunt.' [1]

SERVIUS, Commentary on the Æneid, Bk. vi, l. 378

'A shelfy Coast,
Long infamous for Ships, and Sailors lost;
And white with Bones':

Dryden's Virgil.

---

[1] Soon the Oracle gave this answer to the Lucanians, who were suffering from an epidemic: 'The shade of Palinurus must be appeased!' Whereupon they dedicated to him not far from Velia, a Cenotaph and a Sacred Grove.

INTRODUCTION

It is nearly ten years since *The Unquiet Grave* was begun, long enough for a book to cease to be contemporary and to start settling down to a position in time. With this new and revised edition, an opportunity is presented to show how and why it came to be written and to take on its present form. This may answer some of the criticisms to which Palinurus has not had a chance to reply; such as that *The Unquiet Grave* is merely an anthology, a collection of extracts chosen with 'outremer' snobbery and masquerading as a book or that, if book it be, then it is both morbid and depressing.

The Unquiet Grave is inevitably a war-book. Although the author tried to extricate himself from the war and to escape from his time and place into the bright empyrean of European thought, he could not long remain above the clouds. He was an editor living in Bedford Square who kept a journal in three little note-books provided by his wise printer between the autumn of 1942 and the autumn of 1943. As a man, he was suffering from a private grief,—a separation for which he felt to blame; as an editor, he was struggling against propaganda (the genial guidance of thought by the state which undermines the love of truth and beauty); as a Londoner, he was affected by the dirt and weariness, the gradual draining away under war conditions of light and colour from the former capital of the world and, lastly, as a European, he was acutely aware of being cut off from France. And so in keeping a journal for what a Russian peasant would have called his 'back thoughts,' he was determined to quote as many passages as he could from the French to show the affinity between their thought and ours, and to prove how near and necessary to us were the minds and culture of those across the channel who then seemed quite cut off from us, perhaps for ever. To evoke a French beach at that time was to be reminded that beaches did not exist for mines and pill-boxes and barbed wire but for us to bathe from and that, one day, we would enjoy them again.

We must understand the author's obsession with pleasure at a time when nearly all pleasures were forbidden. Besides his love of France, Palinurus also wished to proclaim his faith in the unity and continuity of Western culture in its moment of crisis. He chose his quotations to illustrate how we have gone on thinking the same things since the days of the ancient Greeks, how the present can always be illuminated by the past. He looked for sanctions rather than originality.

Meanwhile the three notebooks filled up, while the personal sorrow came to a head and disappeared into a long false lull, like an illness. Working on the manuscript for another year, Palinurus began to see that there was a pattern to be brought out; in the diaries an art-form slumbered,—an initiation, a descent into hell, a purification and cure. The various themes could be given symphonic structure and be made to lead into and suggest each other until every paragraph became fitted into an inevitable position in the pilot's periplus (or intellectual voyage) from which it could not be moved. Stained by the juice of time, the second autumn was not quite like the first; the returns of grief or pleasure or religion acquired a richer orchestration, the writing had developed the writer. There was so much to cut or to improve; the exploration of the Palinurus myth (which is mentioned incidentally in the first article the author published) led on to others, until one seemed always to

xii

be pursuing some new clue. It seemed also the moment to collate once and for all the findings of depth-psychology with subjective feelings even if a loss to literature were the result. Finally the whole book had to be re-set. *The Unquiet Grave* by now consisted of thirty long galley-proofs scissored into little pieces like a string of clown's black sausages, covered with insertions and deletions and spread out on the floor to be arranged and re-arranged into a mosaic. The coils of print seemed to move with a life of their own. With incomparable devotion, Lys Lubbock and Sonia Brownell, the two secretaries at *Horizon*, had typed the whole manuscript out twice and at last it was published from here in December 1944 with four collotype plates in a limited edition of a thousand. Lys and Sonia sold copies over the counter, the demand grew and the expenses of the two printings were recovered. The identity of the author-publisher was never regarded as a top secret. By publishing the book without his name, however, more reality was given to the Palinurus myth and the anonymity acted as a coat of varnish to protect what might otherwise seem too personal a confession.

The plot of the book is contained in the title. *The Unquiet Grave* first suggests the tomb of Palinurus, pilot of Æneas; it is the cenotaph from which he haunts us. 'The ghost of Palinurus must be appeased'. He is the core of melancholy and guilt that works destruction on us from within. But the title is also that of an old border ballad in which a lover haunts the grave of his mistress and troubles her sleep.

> 'The wind doth blow tonight, my love,
>   And a few small drops of rain,
>   I never had but one true love,
>   In cold grave she was lain.'

He remains by her grave for a year and a day (the period of the diary) until she dismisses him,

> 'The stalk is withered dry my love,
> So will our hearts decay,
> So make yourself content my love,
> Till God calls you away.

In the first part, Ecce Gubernator ('Behold the pilot'), we are presented with a self-portrait of Palinurus, with his views on literature, love and religion, his bitter doubting attitude. Something is badly wrong; he has lost touch with his sub-conscious self, the well is obstructed; he is reminded of a gull fouled with oil. The presiding genius of this section is Pascal whose terrible sayings penetrate the mask and cause Palinurus to reveal himself and so allude for the first time to his private sorrow, 'Revisit pale Chelsea's nook-shotten Cythera'. Cythera was the Island of love, Shakespeare's word 'nook-shotten' can mean full of indentations, the 'shelfy coast' of the title-page or else full of nooks and alcoves. There follows the first allusion to Paris, 'lost love, lost youth, lost Paris; remorse and folly. Aïe!' Pascal and Leopardi dominate because when they died they were the same age as Palinurus (thirty-nine). Will he survive them? After considering opium as a remedy the pilot continues his downward rush towards the notion of suicide with which the section ends. 'Te Palinure Petens' (looking for you, Palinurus) begins with the worst period of the nightmare journey. The names of four friends who took their own lives are evoked, one, who shoots herself at this very moment, was the companion of the 'dark face' from the Ile-Saint-Louis, most sacred of the holy places. Palinurus is soon driven to admit that all his trouble comes from Paris, and he mentions the Rue Delambre, the Quai d'Anjou (on the Island) and the Rue de Vaugirard as connected with his
xiv

deepest feelings. Two new Genii preside over this section, Sainte-Beuve and Chamfort who bring respectively philosophic resignation and cynical courage to dispel the pessimism of Pascal and Leopardi or the suicidal raving of Nerval. On page 62 comes the first ray of hope. 'Streets of Paris, pray for me; beaches in the sun, pray for me; ghosts of the Lemurs, intercede for me; plane-tree and laurel-rose, shade me; summer rain on quais of Toulon, wash me away.' In the last section this prayer is literally answered. The title 'La clé des chants' (the key to the songs) also suggests Grandville's 'la clé des champs.' The nature-cure. The ferrets and lemurs who represent the strength and beauty of the healthy libido as well as the innocent paradise, the happy pagan honeymoon of the doomed relationship make their appearance in a kind of litany. Here the presiding genius is Flaubert who enriches the sensibility and stoical courage which he shares with the others, with the joy of creation.

Baudelaire, one-time dweller in the Ile-Saint-Louis, also haunts this section and their mutual friend Sainte-Beuve makes a farewell appearance.

The last movement opens with a series of alternating passages on the theme 'Streets of Paris', recalled by autumn mist in London, and 'Beaches in the sun' suggested by the late summer radiance. Mediterranean harbour scenes are followed by Atlantic sea-scapes, with allusions to Baudelaire at Honfleur, Proust at Houlgate and Flaubert at Trouville, where he met his 'fantôme' and dark inspirer, Madame Schlesinger. About the fortieth birthday of Palinurus the catharsis occurs; he re-lives the early stages of his love-affair: the walk to the apartment on the Ile-Saint-Louis, the Paris of the ex-patriates, and the year in the South of France, the villa *Les Lauriers Roses*. Describing this Paradise Lost brings Eden up from the dark world of the sub-conscious where it has been festering into the daylight of art. The ghosts are laid and the avenging 'Lemures' become the affectionate lemurs, until the book closes with a long and reasoned apology for the pursuit of happiness, an affirmation of the values of humanism. Placated and placating, the soul of Palinurus drifts away; his body is washed up on a favourite shore. The epilogue, a pastiche of psycho-analytical jargon and Jungian exegesis, relieves the tension while closely examining the background of the myth. The index will help to identify quotations and to suggest the themes and variations of the story.

As a signal of distress from one human being to another *The Unquiet Grave* went unanswered, but the suffering was alleviated. As a demonstration of the power of words, however, of the obsessional impetus in an aesthetic form to fulfil its destiny, the work was an object-lesson. All grief, once made known to the mind, can be cured by the mind, the manuscript proclaimed; the human brain, once it is fully functioning, as in the making of a poem, is outside time and place and immune from sorrow. 'La pensée console de tout'. If *The Unquiet Grave*, therefore, should leave an impression of being morbid and gloomy then its intention has not been fulfilled.

Cyril Connolly

London
December 1950

PART I

ECCE GUBERNATOR

THE more books we read, the clearer it becomes that the true function of a writer is to produce a masterpiece and that no other task is of any consequence. Obvious though this should be, how few writers will admit it, or having drawn the conclusion, will be prepared to lay aside the piece of iridescent mediocrity on which they have embarked! Writers always hope that their next book is going to be their best, and will not acknowledge that they are prevented by their present way of life from ever creating anything different.

Every excursion into journalism, broadcasting, propaganda and writing for the films, however grandiose, will be doomed to disappointment. To put our best into these is another folly, since thereby we condemn good ideas as well as bad to oblivion. It is in the nature of such work not to last, and it should never be undertaken. Writers engrossed in any literary task which is not an assault on perfection are their own dupes and, unless these self-flatterers are content to dismiss such activity as their contribution to the war effort, they might as well be peeling potatoes.

'Les plus forts y ont péri. L'art est un luxe; il veut des mains blanches et calmes. On fait d'abord une petite concession, puis deux, puis vingt. On s'illusionne sur sa moralité pendant longtemps. Puis on s'en fout complètement et puis on devient imbécile.'—FLAUBERT.

THE UNQUIET GRAVE

Poets arguing about wartime poetry: jackals snarling over a dried-up well.

How many books did Renoir write on how to paint?

To fashion a golden book, to weave a suit that will last some hundred years, it is necessary to feel, to think, and to write. These three activities must be co-ordinated. 'Bien écrire c'est à la fois bien sentir, bien penser et bien dire.'—BUFFON.

We cannot think if we have no time to read, nor feel if we are emotionally exhausted, nor out of cheap material create what is permanent. We cannot co-ordinate what is not there.

What is a masterpiece? Let me name a few. The *Odes* and *Epistles* of Horace, the *Eclogues* and *Georgics* of Virgil, the *Testament* of Villon, the Essays of Montaigne, the Fables of La Fontaine, the Maxims of La Rochefoucauld and La Bruyére, the *Fleurs du Mal* and Intimate Journals of Baudelaire, the Poems of Pope and Leopardi, the *Illuminations* of Rimbaud, and Byron's *Don Juan*.

Such a catalogue reveals the maker. What is common in thought to these twelve writers? Love of life and nature; lack of belief in the idea of progress; interest in, mingled with contempt for humanity. All are what Palinurus has been called by a critic: 'Earthbound'! Yet all are more adult and less romantic than he. These masterpieces then, (mostly high peaks of the secondary range), reflect either what he would like to be, or a self to which he is afraid of confessing. He would like to have written *Les Fleurs du Mal* or the *Saison en Enfer* without being Rimbaud or Baudelaire, that is without undergoing their mental suffering and without being diseased and poor.

In feeling, these works of art contain the maximum of emotion compatible with a classical sense of form.

Observe how they are written; many are short and compressed, fruit of reflective and contemplative natures, prose or poetry of great formal beauty and economy of phrase. There are no novels, plays or biographies included in the list and the poetry is of a kind which speculates about life. They have been chosen by one who most values the art which is distilled and crystallized out of a lucid, curious and passionate imagination. All these writers enjoy something in common, 'jusqu'au sombre plaisir d'un cœur mélancolique': a sense of perfection and a faith in human dignity, combined with a tragic apprehending of our mortal situation, and our nearness to the Abyss.

We can deduce then that the compiler should set himself to write after these models. However unfavourable the conditions for the birth of a classic, he can at least attempt to work at the same level of intention as the Sacred Twelve. Spiritualize the Earthbound, Palinurus, and don't aim too high!

What follow are the doubts and reflections of a year, a word-cycle in three or four rhythms; art, love, nature and religion: an experiment in self-dismantling, a search for the obstruction which is blocking the flow from the well and whereby the name of Palinurus is becoming an archetype of frustration.

As we grow older we discover that what seemed at the time an absorbing interest or preoccupation which we had taken up and thrown over, was in reality an appetite or passion which had swept over us and passed on, until at last we come to see that our life has no more continuity than a pool in the rocks filled by the tide with foam and flotsam and then emptied. Nothing remains of the self but the sediment which this flux

3

deposits; ambergris valuable only to those who know its use.

'Dry again?' said the Crab to the Rock-Pool. 'So would you be,' replied the Rock-Pool, 'if you had to satisfy, twice a day, the insatiable sea.'

As we grow older, in fact, we discover that the lives of most human beings are worthless except in so far as they contribute to the enrichment and emancipation of the spirit. However attractive in our youth the animal graces may seem, if by our maturity they have not led us to emend one character in the corrupt text of existence, then our time has been wasted. No one over thirty-five is worth meeting who has not something to teach us,—something more than we could learn by ourselves, from a book.

LOVE AND ANXIETY

A lover's warning:

'The sixth age is ascribed to Jupiter, in which we begin to take account of our time, to judge of ourselves, and grow to the perfection of our understanding; the last and seventh age to Saturn, wherein our days are sad and overcast and in which we find by dear and lamentable experience, and by the loss which can never be repaired, that of all our vain passions and affections past, the sorrow only abideth.'—SIR WALTER RALEIGH.

There is no pain equal to that which two lovers can inflict on one another. This should be made clear to all who contemplate such a union. The avoidance of this pain is the beginning of wisdom, for it is strong enough to contaminate the rest of our lives: and since it can be minimized by obeying a few simple rules, rules which approximate to Christian marriage, they provide, even to the unbeliever, its *de facto* justification. It is when we begin to hurt those whom we love that the guilt with which we are born becomes intolerable, and since all those whom we love intensely and continuously grow part of us, and as we hate ourselves in them, so we torture ourselves and them together.

The object of Loving is a release from Love. We achieve this through a series of unfortunate love affairs or, without a death-rattle, through one that is happy.

Complete physical union between two people is the rarest sensation which life can provide—and yet not quite real, for it stops when the telephone rings. Such a passion can be maintained at full strength only by the admixture of more unhappiness (jealousy, rows, renunciation) or more and more artificiality (alcohol and other technical illusions). Who escapes this heaven may never have lived, who exists for it alone is soon extinguished.

We pay for vice by the knowledge that we are wicked: we pay for pleasure when we find out, too late, that we are disappearing.

'Pleasure seizes the whole man who addicts himself to it, and will not give him leisure for any good office in life which contradicts the gaiety of the present hour. You may indeed observe in people of pleasure a certain complacency and absence of all severity, which the habit of a loose and unconcerned life gives them; but tell the man of pleasure your secret wants, cares, or sorrows, and you will find that he has given up the delicacy of his passions to the craving of his appetites.'— STEELE.

Beneath a mask of selfish tranquillity nothing exists except bitterness and boredom. I am one of those whom suffering has made empty and frivolous: each night in my dreams I pull the scab off a wound; each day, vacuous and habit-ridden, I help it re-form.

When I contemplate the accumulation of guilt and remorse which, like a garbage-can, I carry through life, and which is fed not only by the lightest action but by the most harmless pleasure, I feel Man to be of all living things the most biologically incompetent and ill-organized. Why has he acquired a seventy-years' life-span only to poison it incurably by the mere being of himself? Why has he thrown Conscience, like a dead rat, to putrefy in the well?

It is no answer to say that we are meant to rid ourselves of the self: religions like Christianity and Buddhism are desperate stratagems of failure, the failure of men to be men. As escapes from the problem, as flights from guilt, they may be welcome, but they cannot turn out to be the revelation of our destiny. What should we think of dogs' monasteries, hermit cats, vegetarian tigers? Of birds who tore off their wings or bulls weeping with remorse? Surely it is in our nature to realize ourselves, yet there remains the deadly flaw by which we feel most guilty when we are most confidently human and are most to be pitied when most successful. Is this because Christianity is true? Or is it an ungrained effect of propaganda for the under-dog? When did the ego begin to stink? Those of us who were brought up as Christians and have lost our faith have retained the sense of sin without the saving belief in redemption. This poisons our thought and so paralyses us in action.

Communism is the new religion which denies original sin, though seldom do we meet a real Communist who seems either complete or happy. And yet Original Sin, what rubbish! The Expulsion from Eden is an act of vindictive womanish spite; the Fall of Man, as recounted in the Bible, comes nearer to the Fall of God.

When I consider what I believe, which I can do only by proceeding from what I do not, I seem in a minority of one,—and yet I know that there are thousands like me: Liberals without a belief in progress, Democrats who despise their fellow-men, Pagans who must live by Christian morals, Intellectuals who cannot find the intellect sufficient,—unsatisfied Materialists, we are as common as clay.

But there can be no going back to Christianity nor can I inhabit an edifice of truth which seems built upon a base of falsehood. The contradictions will out; hence the terrible record of the Church, which 'brings not peace, but a sword'—her persecutions, her cupidity, her hypocrisy, her reaction. These are inherent in her nature as a jealous, worldly, and dogmatic body; and because of these the Church; whenever strong enough to do so, has always belied her spiritual claims.

How privileged are Mahommedans! Small wonder there are more of them than of any other religion and that they are still making converts; for their creed is extro-verted,—the more fanatical they become, the faster they relieve themselves by killing other people. They observe a dignified ritual, a congenial marriage code and appear to be without the sense of guilt.

In my religion all believers would stop work at sundown and have a drink together 'pour chasser la honte du jour.' This would be taken in remembrance of the first sunset when man must have thought the oncoming night would prove eternal, and in honour of the gift of wine to Noah as a relief from the abysmal boredom of the brave new world after the flood. Hence the institution of my 'Sundowner' with which all believers, whether acquainted or not, would render holy that moment of nostalgia and evening apprehension. *Brevis hic est fructus homullis.* In my religion there would be no exclusive doctrine; all would be love, poetry and doubt. Life would be sacred, because it is all we have and death, our common denominator, the fountain of consideration. The Cycle of the Seasons would be rhythmically celebrated together with the Seven Ages of Man, his Identity with all living things, his glorious Reason, and his sacred Instinctual Drives.

Ah, see how on lonely airfield and hill petrol-station the images of Freud and Frazer are wreathed in flowers! From Wabash to Humber the girls are launching their fast-perishing gardens of Adonis far out on to the stream; with sacred rumbas and boogie-woogies the Id is being honoured in all the Hangars, the Priestess intones long passages of the liturgy to which it is most partial; boastful genealogies and anecdotes of the Pornocrats, voodoo incantations, oceans of gibberish from Maldoror and Finnegans Wake! In a rapture of kisses the river-gods return, till Pan and Priapus in their red bowler-hats give way to Human Reason, Human Reason to Divine Love, 'Caelestis Venus', and Divine Love to the gyrations of the Planets through the bright selfless wastes of the Aether.

'The ideal, cheerful, sensuous, pagan life is not sick or sorry. No; yet its natural end is the sort of life which Pompeii and Herculaneum bring so vividly before us,— a life which by no means in itself suggests the thought of horror and misery, which even, in many ways, gratifies the senses and the understanding; but by the very

8

intensity and unremittingness of its appeal to the senses and the understanding, by its stimulating a single side of us too absolutely, ends by fatiguing and revolting us; ends by leaving us with a sense of confinement, of oppression,—with a desire for an utter change, for clouds, storms, effusion and relief.'—MATTHEW ARNOLD.

This argument is often used against Paganism. It is no more true to say that Pompeii and Herculaneum express what is finest in paganism, than that Blackpool and Juan-les-Pins represent the best in Christianity. A life based on reason will always require to be balanced by an occasional bout of violent and irrational emotion, for the instinctual drives must be satisfied. In the past this gratification was provided by the mystery religions, somewhat grossly by the cults of the Great Mother, more spiritually by the Eleusinian and Orphic mysteries. Where Apollo reigns, Dionysus will follow.

Ancestor, my old incarnation, O *Palinurus Vulgaris*, the Venetian red crawfish, langouste, or rock-lobster, whether feeding on the spumy Mauretanian Banks, or undulating —southward to Teneriffe, northward to Scilly—in the systole and diastole of the wave: free me from guilt and fear, free me from guilt and fear, dapple-plated scavenger of the resounding sea!

My previous incarnations: a melon a lobster, a lemur, a bottle of wine, Aristippus.

Periods when I lived: the Augustan age in Rome, in Paris and London from 1660 to 1740, and lastly from 1770 to 1850.

My friends in the first were Horace, Tibullus, Petronius and Virgil; in the second: Rochester, Congreve, La

9

Fontaine, La Bruyère, La Rochefoucauld, Saint Evre-
mond, Dryden, Halifax, Pope, Swift, Racine, Hume,
Voltaire; while in the last avatar I frequented Walpole
and Gibbon; Byron, Fox, Beckford, and Stendhal,
Tennyson, Baudelaire, Nerval and Flaubert.—Afternoons at Holland House, dinners chez Magny.

There are some fruits which awaken in me feelings
deeper than appetite. When I contemplate the musky
golden orb of the sugar-melon or the green and brown
seaweed markings of the tiger cantaloup, the scales of
the pine-apple or the texture of figs and nectarines, the
disposition of oranges and lemons on the tree or the
feign-death coils of the old vine-serpent, I swell in
unity with them, I ripen with the ripe sugar-cane, the
banana in flower, I graft myself on certain trees,—the
stone or umbrella-pine, the sun-loving Norfolk Island
pine, the leaning bamboo, the squat carob, the rusty
cork-oak and the plane. For the hundredth time I
remark with wonder how the leaves and sprays of the
plane-tree forge the pendulous signature of the vine!
'Evincet ulmos platanus coelebs.' The bachelor plane
shall drive out the elms. . . .

My desire is for wisdom, not for the exercise of
the will. 'The will is the strong blind man who
carries on his shoulders the lame man who can see.'—
SCHOPENHAUER.

For me success in life means survival. I believe that a
ripe old age is nature's reward to those who have grasped
her secret. I do not wish to die young or mad. The true
pattern of existence can best be studied in a long life
like Goethe's,—a life of reason interrupted at intervals
by emotional outbursts, displacements, passions, follies.
In youth the life of reason is not in itself sufficient;
10

afterwards the life of emotion, except for short periods, becomes unbearable.

Sometimes at night I get a feeling of claustrophobia; of being smothered by my own personality, of choking through being in the world. During these moments the universe seems a prison wherein I lie fettered by the chains of my senses and blinded through being myself.

It is like being pinned underneath the hull of a capsized boat, yet being afraid to dive deeper and get clear. In those moments it seems that there must be a way out, and that through sloughing off the personality alone can it be taken.

We love but once, for once only are we perfectly equipped for loving: we may appear to ourselves to be as much in love at other times—so will a day in early September, though it be six hours shorter, seem as hot as one in June. And on how that first true love-affair will shape depends the pattern of our lives.

Two fears alternate in marriage, of loneliness and of bondage. The dread of loneliness being keener than the fear of bondage, we get married. For one person who fears being thus tied there are four who dread being set free. Yet the love of liberty is a noble passion and one to which most married people secretly aspire,—in moments when they are not neurotically dependent—but by then it is too late; the ox does not become a bull, nor the hen a falcon.

The fear of loneliness can be overcome, for it springs from weakness; human beings are intended to be free, and to be free is to be lonely, but the fear of bondage is the apprehension of a real danger, and so I find it all the more pathetic to watch young men and beautiful girls taking refuge in marriage from an imaginary danger, a sad loss to their friends and a sore trial to each other. First love is the one most worth having, yet the best marriage is often the second, for we should marry only when the desire for freedom be spent; not till then does a man know whether he is the kind who can settle down. The most tragic breakings-up are of those couples who have married young and who have enjoyed seven years of happiness, after which the banked fires of passion and independence explode—and without knowing why, for they still love each other, they set about accomplishing their common destruction.

When a love-affair is broken off, the heaviest blow is to the vanity of the one who is left. It is therefore reasonable to assume that, when a love-affair is beginning, the greatest source of satisfaction is also to the vanity. The first signs of a mutual attraction will induce even the inconsolable to live in the present.

Cracking tawny nuts, looking out at the tawny planes with their dappled festoons of yellow and green, reading the Tao Tê Ching by a log fire: such is the wisdom of October: autumn bliss; the equinoctial study of religions.

Jesus was a petulant man: his malediction on the barren fig tree was sheer spite, his attitude towards the Pharisees one of paranoiac wrath. He speaks of them as Hitler of the men who made the League of Nations. Those parables which all end 'There shall be wailing and gnashing of teeth',—what a tone for a Redeemer! I find such incidents as the violence used on the man without a wedding garment or the praise of usury in the parable of the talents to be understandable only as outbursts of arrogance and bad temper. Though an inspired genius as a mystic and an ethical reformer, Jesus is also completely a Jew; he does not wish to

12

break away from the Jewish framework of the Old Testament, the Law and the Prophets, but to enrich their ethical content; consequently he imitates the intolerance of the Pharisees whom he condemns ('O ye generation of vipers') and maintains the avenging rôle of God the Father which he claims to have superseded.

Impression of Jesus Christ after re-reading the Gospels: He *thought* he was the son of God, he disliked his parents, was a prig, a high-spirited and serious young man (where was he, what was he doing, between the ages of twelve and twenty-nine?). He felt an especial hatred for the Pharisees, the family, his hometown and adultery, and he may have been illegitimate (Ben Pandere)[1]; he had a macabre sense of humour; was overwhelmingly grateful to those who believed in him ('Thou art Peter'), and extremely close to his elder cousin John, but though moulding himself on him, he was less ascetic. He was fond of wine and very partial to grapes and figs. More civilized than his cousin, he was yet deeply affected by his end, which warned him of what would be his own if he persisted. The death of John and the revelation of Messiahship at Cæsarea

---

[1] The Jewish tradition was that he was the son of a Roman Centurion, Pantheras, the Panther. Hence his aloofness to his 'father' and 'brethren', his ambivalent attitude to his mother and to adultery. (His definition of adultery is very sharp, and he sets 'Thou shalt not commit adultery' as the only commandment beside 'Thou shalt love thy neighbour as thyself'. The question about the woman taken in adultery may have been put to him as a trap by those who believed this story.) I have heard a friend say that the German scholar Von Domaszewski claimed to have found on our Roman Wall the gravestone of Pantheras which showed that his legion had been in Judaea about 4 B.C. The Christians maintained that 'Pantherou', son of the Panther, was a corruption of 'Parthenou', of the Virgin. There is a strange poem by Hardy on this theme.

Philippi completely changed him: impatient, ironical and short-tempered, he was a true faith-healer, inspired by his sublime belief in himself and tragically betrayed by it. I can't believe in his divinity, yet it is impossible not to admire his greatness, his majesty, his fatalistic intuition and that mixture of practical wisdom with sublime vision which alone can save our world. His faith carried him through to the end, then wavered. Was there a secret understanding with John the Baptist? John the Baptist, I feel, holds many clues. About the miracles I suspend judgement. But not about the sermon on the Mount. Those loving dazzling teasing-tender promises are like the lifting of the human horror, the bursting of a great dam. How different he is from Buddha!

Buddha though a philosopher-king is too oriental. His courage in living to a great age, among ageing disciples, confers a pedagogic monotony on his teaching. Besides, we can never absorb his titles; they are ill-accommodated to the Western ear. The Chinese wisdom alone has a natural affinity for the West, the Chinese are always practical. And Tao—a religion without words, without a saviour, without a doubt a God or a future life, whose truth is in a hoof-mark filled with water—what more dare we ask?[1]

'Repose, tranquillity, stillness, inaction—these were the levels of the universe, the ultimate perfection of Tao.'—
CHUANG TZU.

[1] Taoism (pronounced Dowism) is a Monist reconciliation of the human being to the inhuman, inactive harmony of the universe. In return for such an adaption the Taoist resolves his conflict, and gains a sensation of power and tranquillity which he is loth to disturb. His quietism is akin to that of Zeno, Epicurus, Molinos and St. John of the Cross, but dangerously exposed to the corruption of *laisser-aller*.

ECCE GUBERNATOR

Forty,—sombre anniversary to the hedonist,—in seekers
after truth like Buddha, Mahomet, Mencius, St. Ignatius,
the turning-point of their lives.

The secret of happiness (and therefore of success) is
to be in harmony with existence, to be always calm,
always lucid, always willing, 'to be joined to the universe
without being more conscious of it than an idiot', to let
each wave of life wash us a little farther up the shore.

But the secret of art? There have been so many Infernos
and so few Paradises in European art that the Infernos
would seem our true climate. Yet those who have sur-
vived Satanism, war or passion have cared only for
Paradise. In that sense Religion is the sequel to art
and the sequel to love, as *Paradise Regained* follows
half-heartedly after *Paradise Lost*.

Two Modern Taoists

'I have never seen a man who had such creative quiet.
It radiated from him as from the sun. His face was that
of a man who knows about day and night, sky and sea
and air. He did not speak about these things. He had no
tongue to tell of them . . .'
    'I have often seen Klee's window from the street,
with his pale oval face, like a large egg, and his open eyes
pressed to the window pane.'—J. ADLER.

'The only thing in all my experience I cling to is my
coolness and leisurely exhilarated contemplation. If I
could influence you to achieve that *je t'aurais rendu un
peu de service. J'y tiens TELLEMENT—si tu savais
comme j'y tiens*. Let this advice be my perpetual and
most solemn legacy to you.'—W. SICKERT (to Nina
Hamnett).

THE UNQUIET GRAVE

'The mind of the sage in repose becomes the mirror
of the universe, the speculum of all creation.'—
CHUANG TZU.

Whether or not he produce anything, this contemplation is the hall-mark of the artist. It is his gelatine, his
queen-bee jelly, the compost round his roots: the
violent are drawn to such a man by the violence of his
serenity.

'Points upon which the Yellow Emperor doubted, how
can Confucius know?' [1]

Palinurus says: 'It is better to be the lichen on a rock
than the President's carnation. Only by avoiding the
beginning of things can we escape their ending.' Thus
every friendship closes in the quarrel which is a conflict
of wills, and every love-affair must reach a point where
it will attain marriage, and be changed, or decline it,
and wither.

The friendships which last are those wherein each
friend respects the others' dignity to the point of not
wanting anything from him. Therefore a man with
a will to power can have no friends. He is like a boy with
a chopper. He tries it on flowers, then on sticks, then
on furniture, and at last he breaks it on a stone.

There cannot be a personal God without a pessimistic
religion. A personal God is a disappointing God; and
Job, Omar Khayyam, Euripides, Palladas, Voltaire and

---

[1] A proverb which the Taoists coined to discredit their
bustling rival. The Yellow Emperor or Ancestor, revered by
the Taoists, flourished *circa* 2700–2600 B.C. 'The close of his
long reign was made glorious by the appearance of the Phœnix
and the mysterious animal known as the Chi Lin, in token of
his wise and humane administration.'—GILES: *Chinese Biogra-
phical Dictionary.*

Professor Housman will denounce him. With Buddhism, Taoism, Quietism, and the God of Spinoza there can be no disappointment, because there is no Appointment.

Yet no one can achieve Serenity until the glare of passion is past the meridian. There is no certain way of preserving chastity against the will of the body. Lao-Tsu succeeded. But then he was eighty and a Librarian. So he inveighed against books and book-learning, and left but one, shorter than the shortest gospel—a Kaleidoscope of the Void.

Action is the true end of Western religion, contemplation of Eastern; therefore the West is in need of Buddhism (or Taoism or Yoga) and the East of Communism (or muscular Christianity)—and this is just what both are getting. Undergoing the attraction of opposites, we translate the Tao Tê Ching and the Bhagavad-Gita, they learn the Communist Manifesto.

The moment a writer puts his pen to paper he is of his time; the moment he becomes of his time he ceases to appeal to other periods and so will be forgotten. He who would write a book that would last for ever must learn to use invisible ink. Yet if an author is of his age, parallel situations will recur which he may return to haunt. He will obsess the minds of living writers, prevent them from sleeping, crowd them out like the *Horla* and snatch the bread from their mouths.

Our minds do not come of age until we discover that the great writers of the past whom we patronize, dead though they be, are none the less far more intelligent than ourselves—Proust, James, Voltaire, Donne, Lucretius —how we would have bored them!

Fallen leaves lying on the grass in the November sun bring more happiness than daffodils. Spring is a call to action, hence to disillusion, therefore is April called 'the cruellest month'. Autumn is the mind's true Spring; what is there we have, 'quidquid promiserat annus' and it is more than we expected.

WOMEN

There is no fury like an ex-wife searching for a new lover. When we see a woman chewing the cud meekly beside her second husband, it is hard to imagine how brutally, implacably and pettily she got rid of the others. There are two great moments in a woman's life: when first she finds herself to be deeply in love with her man and when she leaves him. Leaving him enables her to be both sadist and masochist, to be stony when he implores her to stay and to weep because she has decided to go. Women differ from men in that to break with the past and mangle their mate in the process fulfils a dark need. Thus a wife's woman-friends will derive an almost equal satisfaction from her impending departure. Together they prepare the brief against the husband which will strip him of his friends. They love to know the date, to fan the flames, and when the Monster is alone to rush round and inspect him. They will hear the clump of suit-cases a hundred streets away.

Beware of a woman with too many girl-friends, for they will always try to destroy the conjugal WE. One girl-friend is worse, unless afterwards we marry her. In America every woman has her set of girl-friends; some are cousins, the rest are gained at school. These form a permanent committee who sit on each other's affairs, who 'come out' together, marry and divorce together, and who end as those groups of bustling, heartless well-informed club-women who govern society. Against them the Couple or Ehepaar is helpless and Man in their eyes but a biological interlude.

18

In the sex-war thoughtlessness is the weapon of the male, vindictiveness of the female. Both are reciprocally generated, but a woman's desire for revenge outlasts all other emotion.

> 'And their revenge is as the tiger's spring,
>   Deadly, and quick, and crushing; yet as real
>   Torture is theirs, what they inflict they fell.'

When every unkind word about women has been said, we have still to admit, with Byron, that they are nicer than men. They are more devoted, more unselfish and more emotionally sincere. When the long fuse of cruelty, deceit and revenge is set alight, it is male thoughtlessness which has fired it.

A woman who will not feign submission can never make a man happy and so never be happy herself. There has never been a happy suffragette. In a perfect union the man and woman are like a strung bow. Who is to say whether the string bend the bow, or the bow tighten the string? Yet male bow and female string are in harmony with each other and an arrow can be fitted. Unstrung, the bow hangs aimless; the cord flaps idly.

A man who has nothing to do with women is incomplete. A puritan is incomplete because he excludes that half of himself of which he is afraid and so the deeper he imprisons himself in his fastidiousness, the more difficulty he has in finding a woman who is brave enough to simulate the vulgarity by which he can be released.

'Sabba dukkha, sabba anatta, sabba anikka.' [1]

[1] 'Sorrow is everywhere
   In man is no abiding entity
   In things no abiding reality.'—BUDDHA ('a dirge that still resounds mournfully in ten thousand monasteries').

A stone lies in a river; a piece of wood is jammed against it; dead leaves, drifting logs, and branches caked with mud collect; weeds settle there, and soon birds have made a nest and are feeding their young among the blossoming water plants. Then the river rises and the earth is washed way. The birds depart, the flowers wither, the branches are dislodged and drift downward; no trace is left of the floating island but a stone submerged by the water;—such is our personality.

If (as Christians, Buddhists, Mystics, Yogis, Platonists, believe), our life is vanity, the world unreal, personality non-existent, the senses deceivers, their perceptions and even reason and imagination false; then how tragic that from the Flesh are such deductions always made! If our mission in life is to evolve spiritually, then why are we provided with bodies so refractory that in many thousands of years we have not been able to improve them? Not one lust of the flesh, not one single illusion, not even our male nipples have been bred out of us; and still our new-born babies roll about in paroxysms of sensual cupidity and egomaniac wrath.

Three faults, which are found together and which infect every activity: laziness, vanity, cowardice. If one is too lazy to think, too vain to do a thing badly, too cowardly to admit it, one will never attain wisdom. Yet it is only the thinking which begins when habit-thinking leaves off, which is ignited by the logic of the train of thought, that is worth pursuing. A comfortable person can seldom follow up an original idea any further than a London pigeon can fly.

Complacent mental laziness is our national disease.

Today our literature is suffering from the decay of poetry and the decline of fiction, yet never have there been so many novelists and poets; this is because neither will overcome the difficulties of their medium. Irresponsible poets who simulate inspiration trample down the flower of a language as brutally as politician and journalist blunt and enfeeble with their slovenliness the common run of words. Many war poets don't try; they are like boys playing about on a billiard table who wonder what the cues and pockets are for. Nor is it easier for novelists, who can no longer develop character, situation or plot.

Flaubert, Henry James, Proust, Joyce and Virginia Woolf have finished off the novel. Now all will have to be re-invented as from the beginning.

Let us reflect whether there be any living writer whose silence we would consider a literary disaster: one who, with three centuries more of art and history to draw from, can sustain a comparison with, for example, Pascal.

Pascal's *Pensées* were written about 1660. Many of them are modern not merely in thought, but in expression and force; they would be of overwhelming importance if they were now published for the first time. Such a genius must invalidate the usual conception of human progress. Particularly modern are his rapidity, detachment and intellectual impatience.

Resemblance. Pascal: Leopardi: Baudelaire.

WISDOM OF PASCAL 1623–1662

'Tout le malheur des hommes vient d'une seule chose, qui est de ne savoir pas demeurer en repos, dans une chambre.'

'Notre nature est dans le mouvement; le repos entier est la mort.'

Ennui: 'Rien n'est si insupportable à l'homme que d'être dans un plein repos, sans passions, sans affaire, sans divertissement, sans application. Il sent alors son néant, son insuffisance, sa dépendance, son impuissance, son vide. Incontinent il sortira du fond de son âme l'ennui, la noirceur, la tristesse, le chagrin, le dépit, le désespoir.'

Misère: 'La seule chose qui nous console de nos misères est le divertissement, et cependant c'est la plus grande de nos misères, car c'est cela qui nous empêche principalement de songer à nous, et qui nous fait perdre insensiblement.'

La Gloire: 'L'admiration gâte tout dès l'enfance: Oh! que cela est bien dit! Oh! qu'il a bien fait! Qu'il est sage, etc. . . .'

'Les enfants de Port-Royal, auxquels on ne donne point cet aiguillon d'envie et de gloire, tombent dans la nonchalance.'

Pascal and Leopardi (both died aged thirty-nine), depress and frighten one because they were ill, almost deformed, and therefore because their deformity renders suspect so much of their pessimism. They are the Grand Inquisitors who break down our alibis of health and happiness. Are they pessimistic because they are ill? Or does their illness act as a short cut to reality—which is intrinsically tragic?[1] Or did their deformities encourage the herd to treat them thoughtlessly, and so create in them a catastrophic impression of human nature?

[1] 'For aught we know to the contrary, 103 or 104 degrees Fahrenheit might be a much more favourable temperature for truths to germinate and sprout in, than the more ordinary blood-heat of 97 or 98 degrees.'—WILLIAM JAMES.

In many of Pascal's reflections one detects not only the scientific accuracy, but the morbidity and peevishness, the *injustice* of Proust.

How was La Rochefoucauld's health?

Pascal's 'moi' is Freud's 'Id'. Thus Pascal writes, 'Le *moi* est haïssable . . . le *moi* a deux qualités: il est injuste en soi, en ce qu'il se fait centre du tout; il est incommode aux autres, en ce qu'il les veut asservir: car chaque *moi* est l'ennemi et voudrait être le tyran de tous les autres'.

This is Freud. But though babies are born *all* 'Id', we do not for that condemn the human race.

We may consider that we are born as 'Id' and that the object of life is to sublimate the 'Id',—the 'Id' is all greed, anger, fear, vanity and lust. Our task is to purge it, to shed it gradually as an insect sheds its larval form.

Life is a maze in which we take the wrong turning before we have learnt to walk.

Pascal says: 'Death should infallibly put them [the pleasure-lovers] very soon in the horrible necessity of being eternally unhappy . . .' We keep forgetting his belief in Hell, because we can accept so much else that he believes. Yet believing in Hell must distort every judgement on this life. However much a Christian may claim that the central doctrine of the Church is the Incarnation and nothing else, he is led on inevitably to exclusive salvation, to Heaven and Hell, to censorship and the persecution of heresy, till he finds himself among the brothel-owning Jesuits and cannon-blessing bishops of the Spanish war.

Pascal (or Hemingway, Sartre, or Malraux).

'Qu'on s'imagine un nombre d'hommes dans les chaînes, et tous condamnés à la mort, dont les uns étant chaque jour égorgés à la vue des autres, ceux qui restent voient leur propre condition dans celle de leurs sem-blables, et, se regardant les uns et les autres avec douleur et sans espérance, attendent à leur tour. C'est l'image de la condition des hommes.'

December 12th: Revisit pale Chelsea's nook-shotten Cythera.

Christmas Eve: Dégoûté de tout. Midwinter cafard.

> La Nochebuena se viene
> la Nochebuena se va
> y nosotros nos iremos
> y no volveremos más.[1]

No opinions, no ideas, no true knowledge of anything, no ideals, no inspiration; a fat slothful, querulous, greedy, impotent carcass; a stump, a decaying belly washed up on the shore. 'Manes Palinuri esse placandos!' Always tired, always bored, always hurt, always hating.

Sacred names: Rue de Chanaleilles. Summer night, limes in flower; old houses, with large gardens enclosed by high walls; silent heart of the leafy Faubourg: sensation of what is lost: lost love, lost youth, lost Paris,—remorse and folly. Aïe!

A love affair is a grafting operation. 'What has once been joined, never forgets.' There is a moment when the graft takes; up to then is possible without difficulty the separation which afterwards comes only through break-ing off a great hunk of oneself, the ingrown fibre of hours, days, years.

---

[1] Christmas eve comes, Christmas eve goes and we too shall pass and never more return. Old Spanish carol.

New-year resolution: lose a stone, then all the rest will follow. Obesity is a mental state, a disease brought on by boredom and disappointment; greed, like the love of comfort, is a kind of fear. The one way to get thin is to re-establish a purpose in life.

Thus a good writer must be in training: if he is a stone too heavy then that fourteen pounds represents for him so much extra indulgence, so much clogging laziness; in fact a coarsening of sensibility. There are but two ways to be a good writer: like Homer, Shakespeare or Goethe, to accept life completely, or like Pascal, Proust, Leopardi, Baudelaire, to refuse ever to lose sight of its horror.

When we reflect on life we perceive that only through solitary communion with nature can we gain an idea of its richness and meaning. We know that in such contemplation lies our true personality, and yet we live in an age when we are told exactly the opposite and asked to believe that the social and co-operative activity of humanity is the one way through which life can be developed. Am I an exception, a herd-outcast? There are also solitary bees, and it is not claimed that they are biologically inferior. A planet of contemplators, each sunning himself before his doorstep like the mason-wasp; no one would help another, and no one would need help!

Marriage: 'An experience everyone should go through and then live his own life' *or* 'living one's own life— an experience everyone should go through and then marry'?

The tragedy of modern marriage is that married couples no longer enjoy the support of society, although marriage, difficult enough at any time, requires social sanction. Thus, in the past, married women censured the unmarried; the constant punished the inconstant; society outlawed the divorced and the dwellers-in-sin. Now it does the opposite. The State harries the human couple and takes both man and wife for its wars, society quests impatiently for the first suspicion of mistress or lover, and neurotic three-in-a-bedders, lonely and envious, make the young ménage their prey.

'In wise love each divines the high secret self of the other, and, refusing to believe in the mere daily self, creates a mirror where the lover or the beloved sees an image to copy in daily life.'—YEATS.

Human life is understandable only as a state of transition, as part of an evolutionary process; we can take it to be a transition between the animal world and some other form which we assume to be spiritual. Anxiety and remorse are the results of failing to advance spiritually. For this reason they follow close on pleasure, which is not necessarily harmful, but which, since it does not bring advancement with it, outrages that part of us which is concerned with growth. Such ways of passing time as chess, bridge, drink and motoring accumulate guilt. But what constitutes the spiritual ideal? Is it the Nietzschean Superman or his opposite, the Buddha? The spiritual trend of human beings would seem to be towards pacifism, vegetarianism, contemplative mysticism, the elimination of violent emotion and even of self-reproduction. But is it impossible to improve animal-man so that instead of being made to renounce his animal nature, he refines it? Can anxiety and remorse be avoided in that way? Imagine a cow or a pig which rejected the body for a 'noble eight-fold way of self-enlightenment'. One would feel that the beast had made a false calculation. If our elaborate and dominating bodies are given us to be denied at every turn, if our nature is always wrong and wicked, how ineffectual we are—like fishes not meant to swim. Have the solitary, the chaste, the ascetic who have been with us now for six thousand years, ever been proved to be right? Has humanity shown any sign of evolving in their direction? As well as Diogenes and the Stylite, there is also Aristippus and Epicurus as alternative to the Beast.[1]

And now we have a new conception: the Group Man. Man's spiritual evolution, about which I prate, taking the form of a leap from the poorly organized wolf-pack and sheep-flock into an insect society, a community in which the individual is not merely a gregarious unit, but a cell in the body itself. Community and individual are, in fact, indistinguishable. How will you enjoy that, Palinurus?

[1] The Middle Way.
'Aristippus parlant à des jeunes gens qui rougissaient de le voir entrer chez une courtisane: "Le vice est de n'en pas sortir, non pas d'y entrer." '—MONTAIGNE (*Essais*, III, v).

A charm against the Group Man

THE MAGIC CIRCLE

Peace-aims: (1) a yellow manor farm inside this magic circle;

(2) a helicopter to take me to

(3) an office in London or Paris and

(4) to my cabin at Almuñecar or Ramatuelle.

ECCE GUBERNATOR

Daydream: A golden classical house, three stories high, with *œil de bœuf* attic windows looking out over water. A magnolia Delavayi growing up the wall, a terrace for winter, a great tree for summer and a lawn for games; a wooded hill behind and a river below, then a sheltered garden, indulgent to fig and nectarine, and at an angle of the wall, a belvedere, book-lined like that of Montaigne, wizard of the magic circle, with this motto from him: 'La liberté et l'oisiveté qui sont mes maîtresses qualités'.

As I waddle along in thick black overcoat and dark suit with a leather brief-case under my arm, I smile to think how this costume officially disguises the wild and storm-tossed figure of Palinurus; who knows that a poet is masquerading here as a whey-faced bureaucrat? And who should ever know?

The secret of happiness lies in the avoidance of Angst (anxiety, spleen, noia, fear, remorse, cafard). It is a mistake to consider happiness as a positive state. By removing Angst, the condition of all unhappiness, we are then prepared to receive such blessings as may come our way. We know very little about Angst, which may even proceed from the birth trauma, or be a primitive version of the sense of original sin, but we can try to find out what makes it worse.[1]

Angst can take the form of remorse about the past, guilt about the present, anxiety about the future. Often

---

[1] Freudians consider anxiety to arise from the repression of anger or love. Kretschmer thinks there is an obscure somatic relation between anxiety and sex. Theologians associate it with the Fall, Behaviorists with undigested food in the stomach, Kierkegaard with the vertigo that precedes sin. Buddha and many philosophers regarded it as concurrent with Desire. Thus Bacon quotes Epicurus: 'Use not that you may not wish, wish not that you may not fear'.

it is due to our acceptance through an imperfect know-ledge of ourselves of conventional habits of living. Thus to keep someone waiting or to be kept waiting is a cause of Angst which is out of all proportion to the minor fault of unpunctuality. Therefore we may assume that we keep people waiting symbolically because we do not wish to see them and that our anxiety is due not to being late, but lest our hostility be deteced. The chroni-cally unpunctual should cancel all engagements for a definite period. Similarly, anxiety at being kept waiting is a form of jealousy, a fear that we are not liked.

Fatigue is one cause of Angst which may disappear if the tired person is able to lie down; bad air is another, or seeing a tube train move out as one reaches the plat-form.

To sit late in a restaurant (especially when one has to pay the bill) or over a long meal after a cocktail party is particularly conducive to Angst, which does not affect us after snacks taken in an armchair with a book. The business lunch is another meal from which we would prefer to be driven away in a coffin. Certainly a frequent cause of Angst is an awareness of the waste of our time and ability, such as may be witnessed among people kept waiting by a hairdresser.

Further considerations on cowardice, sloth and vanity; vices which do small harm to other people but which prevent one from doing any good and which poison and enfeeble all the virtues. Sloth rots the intelligence, cowardice destroys all power at the source, while vanity inhibits us from facing any fact which might teach us something; it dulls all other sensation.

Home Truth from La Bruyère: 'L'expérience confirme que la mollesse ou l'indulgence pour soi et la dureté pour les autres n'est qu'un seul et même vice'.

ECCE GUBERNATOR

I see the world as a kind of Black Hole of Calcutta, where we are all milling about in darkness and slime; now and then the mere being in the world is enough to cause violent claustrophobia (or is it a physical shortness of breath which creates the sensation of claustrophobia and therefore the image of the Black Hole?) And then I know that it is only by some desperate escape, like Pascal's, that I can breathe; but cowardice and sloth prevent me from escaping.

Who have escaped?
'Those who know don't speak;
Those who speak don't know.'

On the American desert are horses which eat loco-weed and some are driven mad by it; their vision is affected, they take enormous leaps to cross a tuft of grass or tumble blindly into rivers. The horses which have become thus addicted are shunned by the rest and will never rejoin the herd. So is it with human beings: those who are conscious of another world, the world of the spirit, acquire an outlook which distorts the values of ordinary life; they are consumed by the weed of non-attachment. Curiosity is their one excess and therefore they are recognized not by what they do but by what they refrain from doing, like those Araphants or disciples of Buddha who were pledged to the 'Nine Incapabilities'. Thus they do not take life, they do not compete, they do not boast, they do not join groups of more than six, they do not condemn others; they are 'abandoners of revels, mute, contemplative' who are depressed by gossip, gaiety and equals, who wait to be telephoned to, who neither speak in public nor keep up with their friends nor take revenge on their enemies. Self-knowledge has taught them to abandon hate and blame and envy in their lives until they look sadder than they are.

They seldom make positive assertions because they see, outlined against any statement, (as a painter sees a complementary colour), the image of its opposite. Most psychological questionnaires are designed to search out these moonlings and ensure their non-employment. They divine each other by a warm indifference for they know that they are not intended to foregather, but, like stumps of phosphorus in the world's wood, each to give forth his misleading radiance.

The two errors: We can either have a spiritual or a materialist view of life. If we believe in the spirit then we make an assumption which permits a whole chain down to a belief in fairies, witches, astrology, black magic, ghosts, and treasure-divining; the point at which we stop believing is dictated by our temperament or by our mood at a given moment. Thus the early Christians believed in the miracles of false prophets, and regarded the pagan gods as devils who had entrenched themselves in secure positions. They were more pagan than I am. On the other hand a completely materialist view leads to its own excesses, such as a belief in Behaviorism, in the economic basis of art, in the social foundation of ethics and the biological nature of psychology, in fact to the justification of expediency and therefore ultimately to the Ends-Means fallacy of which our civilization is perishing.

If we believe in a supernatural or superhuman intelligence creating the universe, then we end by stocking our library with the prophecies of Nostradamus and the calculations on the Great Pyramid. If instead we choose to travel viâ Montaigne and Voltaire, then we choke among the brimstone aridities of the Left Book Club.
It is a significant comment on the victory of science over magic that were someone to say 'if I put this pill

in your beer it will explode,' we might believe them; but were they to cry 'if I pronounce this spell over your beer it will go flat,' we should remain incredulous and Paracelsus, the Alchemists, Aleister Crowley and all the Magi have lived in vain. Yet when I read science I turn magical; when I study magic, scientific.

We cannot say that truth lies in the centre between the spiritual and material conception, since life must be one thing or the other. But can it be both? Supposing life were created by an act of God willing the accidental combination of chemicals to form a cell; created in fact by deliberate accident. Then, in the confidence of youth when the body seems self-sufficing, it would be natural to emphasize the materialist nature of phenomena, and in old age, when the body begins to betray us, to abandon our sensual outlook for a more spiritual cosmorama,—and both times we should be right.

Sunshine streams through the room, the dove grinds her love-song on the roof, out in the square the grass turns green, the earth has been cleared round the daffodils as a stage is cleared for the dancers, and under a rinsed blue sky the streets remember Canaletto; London spring is on its way.

Spring, season of massacre and offensives, of warm days and flowing blood, of flowers and bombs. Out with the hyacinths, on with the slaughter! Glorious weather for tanks and land-mines!

The creative moment of a writer comes with the autumn. The winter is the time for reading, revision, preparation of the soil; the spring for thawing back to life; the summer is for the open air, for satiating the body with health and action, but from October to Christmas for the release of mental energy, the hard crown of the year.

33

The duality of man is the heresy of Paul and Plato, heresy because the concept of soul and body is bound to imply a struggle between them which leads on the one hand to asceticism and puritanism, on the other to excess of materialism and sensuality. The greatness of Christ and Buddha sprang from the abandonment of asceticism for the Middle Path.

The spiritual life of man is the flowering of his bodily existence: there is a physical life which remains the perfect way of living for natural man, a life in close contact with nature, with the sun and the passage of the seasons, and one rich in opportunities for equinoctial migrations and home-comings. This life has now become artificial, out of reach of all but the rich or the obstinately free, yet until we can return to it we are unable to appreciate the potentialities of living. (Whales, branded in the Arctic, are found cruising in Antarctic waters; men, ringed in childhood, are observed, seventy years later, under the same stone.) We may compare a human being to a fruit-tree whose purpose is its fruit, fruit out of all proportion to the tree's value; yet, unless the tree receives its years of leisure, its requirements of sun and rain, the fruit will not ripen. So it is with the spiritual virtues of man, for we have divided man into two kinds; those whose soil is so poor or the climate of whose lives so unsuitable that they can never bear, or those who are forced and cramped under glass, whose lives are so constricted by responsibility that they become all fruit; hasty, artificial and without flavour.

We progress through an intensifying of the power generated by the physical satisfaction of natural man, whose two worst enemies are apathy and delirium; the apathy which spreads outward from the mechanical life, the delirium which results from the violent methods we use to escape.

34

Happiness lies in the fulfilment of the spirit through the body. Thus humanity has already evolved from an animal life to one more civilized. There can be no complete return to nature, to nudism or desert-islandry: city life is the subtlest ingredient in the human climate. But we have gone wrong over the size of our cities and over the kind of life we lead in them; in the past the clods were the peasants, now the brute mass of ignorance is urban. The village idiot walks in Leicester Square. To live according to nature we should pass a considerable time in cities for they are the glory of human nature, but they should never contain more than two hundred thousand inhabitants; it is our artificial enslavement to the large city, too sprawling to leave, too enormous for human dignity, which is responsible for half our sickness and misery. Slums may well be breeding-grounds of crime, but middle-class suburbs are incubators of apathy and delirium. No city should be too large for a man to walk out of in a morning.[1]

Surrealism is a typical city-delirium movement, a violent explosion of urban claustrophobia; one cannot imagine Surrealists except in vast cities, 'paysans de Paris' or New York. The nihilism of Céline and Miller is another by-product, and so are those mass-movers, Marx with his carbuncles, Hitler with his Beer-Hall. The English masses are lovable: they are kind, decent, tolerant, practical and not stupid. The tragedy is that there are too many of them, and that they are aimless, having outgrown the servile functions for which they were encouraged to multiply. One day these huge crowds will have to seize power because there will be

[1] 'We are not yet ripe for growing up in the streets . . . has any good ever come out of the foul-clustering town-proletariat, beloved of humanitarians? Nothing—never; they are only waiting for a leader, some 'inspired idiot' to rend to pieces our poor civilization.'—NORMAN DOUGLAS: *Siren Land*, 1911.

35

nothing else for them to do, and yet they neither demand power nor are ready to make use of it; they will learn only to be bored in a new way. Sooner or later the population of England will turn Communist, and then take over. Some form of State Socialism is the only effective religion for the working class; its coming is therefore as inevitable as was that of Christianity. The Liberal Die-hard then grows to occupy historically the same position as the 'good Pagan': he is doomed to extinction.

While we re-live the horrors of the Dark Ages, of absolute States and ideological wars, the old platitudes of liberalism loom up in all their glory, familiar streets as we reel home furious in the dawn.

Wisdom of de Quincey
de Quincey: decadent English essayist who, at the age of seventy-five, was carried off by half a century of opium-eating.

'Marriage had corrupted itself through the facility of divorce and through the consequences of that facility (viz. levity in choosing and fickleness in adhering to the choice) into so exquisite a traffic of selfishness that it could not yield so much as a phantom model of sanctity.'

'By the law I came to know sin.'

On the first time he took opium in 1804: 'It was Sunday afternoon, wet and cheerless; and a duller spectacle this earth of ours has not to show than a rainy Sunday in London.'

The mystery of drugs: How did savages all over the world, in every climate, discover in frozen tundras or remote jungles the one plant, indistinguishable from so many others of the same species, which could, by a most elaborate process, bring them fantasies, intoxication, and freedom from care? How unless by help from the plants themselves? Opium-smokers in the East become surrounded by cats, dogs, birds and even spiders, who are attracted by the smell. The craving for the drug proceeds from the brain-cells which revolt and overrule the will. The Siberian tribes who eat Agaric say, 'The Agaric orders me to do this or that'— the Hashish chewers experience a like sensation. Horses and cattle which become 'indigo eaters' continue to gorge till they drop dead. Though one of the rarest and most obscure drugs, Peotl gave its name to a range of uninhabited mountains where it is found.

The Greeks and Romans looked on alcohol and opium as lovely twin reconcilers to living and dying presented to man by Dionysus and Morpheus,—God-given because of their extraordinary sympathy to us and because of the mystery attending their discovery. If man be part of nature, then his parasites may well understand him better than he knows.

Since there are flowers whose fertilization is impossible except by means of an insect, flowers which eat insects and therefore understand them, since so low and unconscious an order has these correspondences with the one above, may there not be animals and birds who make use of man and study his habits and if they do, why not insects and vegetables? What grape, to keep its place in the sun, taught our ancestors to make wine?

Everything is a dangerous drug to me except reality, which is unendurable. Happiness is in the imagination. What we perform is always inferior to what we imagine; yet day-dreaming brings guilt; there is no happiness except through freedom from Angst and only creative work, communion with nature and helping others are Anxiety-free.

Fraternity is the State's bribe to the individual; it is the one virtue which can bring courage to members of a materialist society. All State propaganda exalts comradeship for it is this gregarious herd-sense and herd-smell which keep people from thinking and so reconcile them to the destruction of their private lives. A problem for government writers or for the war artists in their war cemeteries: how to convert Fraternity into an æsthetic emotion?

Subversive thought for the year: 'Every man is to be respected as an absolute end in himself; and it is a crime against the dignity that belongs to him to use him as a mere means to some external purpose.'—KANT.

'If I had to choose between betraying my country and betraying my friend, I hope I should have the guts to betray my country.' This statement by Mr. E. M. Forster reminds us how far we have wandered from the ancient conception of friendship, of treating a kindred soul as an end not a means. 'The Chinese poet recommends himself as a friend, the Western poet as a lover,' writes Arthur Waley; but the Western prose-writer also used to recommend himself as a friend; the seventeenth and eighteenth centuries elaborated friendship and all but made it their religion. In the circle of Johnson, of Walpole and Madame du Deffand or of the Encyclopædists nobody could live without his friend. They loved them and even a misanthropic philosopher like La Bruyère could grow sentimental over the theme. Only the invalid Pascal demolished friendship on the ground that if we could read each other's thoughts it would disappear.

Now the industrialization of the world, the totalitarian State, and the egotism of materialism have made an end to friendship; the first through speeding up the tempo of human communication to the point where no one is indispensable, the second by making such demands on the individual that comradeship can be practised between workers and colleagues only for the period of their co-operation and the last by emphasizing whatever is fundamentally selfish and nasty in people, so that we are unkind about our friends and resentful of their intimacy because of something which is rotting in ourselves. We have developed sympathy at the expense of loyalty.

How many people drop in on us? That is a criterion of friendship. Or may tell us our faults? To how many do we give unexpected presents? With whom can we remain silent? The egocentric personality requires, alas, a changing audience, not a constant scrutiny. Romantic lovers are disloyal and, by making fun of old friends, they hit upon a congenial way of entertaining each other.

Voltaire on Friendship: 'C'est un contrat tacite entre deux personnes sensibles et vertueuses. Je dis *sensibles* car un moine, un solitaire peut n'étre point méchant et vivre sans connaître l'amitié. Je dis *vertueuses*, car les méchants n'ont que des complices, les voluptueux ont des compagnons de débauche, les intéressés ont des associés, les politiques assemblent des fâcheux, le commun des hommes oisifs a des liaisons, les princes ont des courtisans: les hommes vertueux ont seuls des amis.' When we see someone living alone, like a beech-tree in a clearing, with no other signs of life around him yet proclaiming his freedom, displaying his possessions and maintaining his devotion to his friends, we can be sure that such a person is an ogre and that human bone-meal lies buried under his roots.

MASTERPLAY

Three requisites for a work of art: validity of the myth, vigour of belief, intensity of vocation. Examples of valid myths: The Gods of Olympus in Ancient Greece; the City of Rome and afterwards the Roman Empire; Christianity; the discovery of Man in the Renaissance with its consequence, the Age of Reason; the myths of Romanticism and of Material Progress (how powerful is the myth of bourgeois life in the work of the Impressionist painters!). The belief in a myth whose validity is diminishing will not produce such great art as the belief in one which is valid, and none are valid today. Yet no myth is ever quite worthless as long as there remains one artist to honour it with his faith.

O for the past, when a masterpiece was enough to maintain a reputation for life! All Catullus, Tibullus and Propertius fit into the same volume; Horace and Virgil require but one tome, so do La Fontaine and La Bruyère. One book for each lifetime and the rest is fame, ease and freedom from Angst. Nature was so indulgent; if we could but write one good book every twelve years we would have done as well as Flaubert. Voltaire wrote *Candide* when he was sixty-five, Peacock wrote *Gryll Grange* at seventy-five, at eighty Joinville began his *Life of St. Louis*. Waste is a law of art as it is of nature. There is always time.

Every good writer must discover the yawning crevasse which separates Man's finite destiny from his infinite potentialities. It is afterwards that he will reveal his artistic courage and so register the protest which is a final plea for order, his *Gulliver's Travels*, his *Maxims*, his *Songs of Experience*, his *Saison en Enfer*, his *Fleurs du Mal*. The rest either pretend that they have seen nothing, and that all is well, or else howl with self-pity.

40

Optimism and self-pity are the positive and negative poles of contemporary cowardice.

What makes the great writers of the past vivid to us is the extent of their misery; the despair of Pascal, the bitterness of La Rochefoucauld, the ennui of Flaubert, the 'noia' of Leopardi, the 'spleen' of Baudelaire,— none but the truths which have been extracted under mental torture appeal to us. We live in so desperate an age that any happiness which we possess must be hidden like a deformity, for we know that, though all our nature revolt, we can create only through what we suffer.

'We are all conceived in close prison . . . and then all our life is but a going out to the place of execution, to death. Nor was there any man seen to sleep in the cart between Newgate and Tyburn—between prison and the place of execution, does any man sleep? But we sleep all the way; from the womb to the grave we are never thoroughly awake.'—DONNE.

A modern Rune: 'Pooey on the war!' No one can pronounce these four words and not feel a tremor of earth-shaking dimension. And not until the two thousand and fifty million belligerents can thunder them in unison, will the war be over.

A Rune for the very bored: When very bored recite: 'It was during the next twenty minutes that there occurred one of those tiny incidents which revolutionize the whole course of our life and alter the face of history. Truly we are the playthings of enormous fates.'

The ten-year torture of two faces. 'The tyranny of the human face.' When we see a friend in the depth of despair because they have been left by someone whom we know to be insignificant, we must remember that there is a way of leaving and yet of not leaving; of hinting that one loves and is willing to return, yet never coming back and so preserving a relationship in a lingering decay. This technique can be learnt like a hold in jiu-jitsu. The person who has been abandoned is always psychologically groggy; the ego is wounded in its most tender part and is forced back on the separation and rejection phobias of infancy. Someone who knows how to prolong this state and to reproduce it at will can be quite insignificant,—so is the sand-wasp which stings a grub in the nerve-centre where it will be paralysed, yet remain alive.

Axiom: There is no happiness to be obtained by the destruction of another's. To take wife away from husband or husband from wife, is a kind of murder; guilt turns lovers into bad accomplices and the wrecking of a home destroys the wreckers. As we leave others, so shall we be left.

There is immunity in reading, immunity in formal society, in office routine, in the company of old friends and in the giving of officious help to strangers, but there is no sanctuary in one bed from the memory of another. The past with its anguish will break through every defence-line of custom and habit; we must sleep and therefore we must dream.

And in our dreams, as in the vacant afternoons of London week-ends, there enter the excluded, the disinherited, the heartbroken, the heart-breakers, the saboteurs and wrecking crews of our daylight selves. Θύραζε κῆρες.[1] Bone-crunching hyenas!

The harbour of Cassis on a bright winter morning; a gull is floating a few yards from the quay, unable to

[1] 'Spectres avaunt!' Ancient Greek spell.

rise because its wings are fouled with oil. The fisher-
children pelt it with stones. I drive them off; laughing
they run across to the farther side and begin again,
the stones falling around the dying bird as it bobs on
the water like a painted decoy.

> 'While under its storm-beaten breast
> Cried out the hollows of the sea.'

Causes of Angst: Angst is inherent in the uncoiling
of the ego, the tapeworm, the *ver solitaire*. It dwells
in the *Lacrimæ Rerum*, in the contrasting of the Past
with the present. It lurks in old loves and old letters
or in our despair at the complexity of modern life.
   Effect: Misery, disgust, tears, guilt.
   Temporary cures: (1) Lunch with a new friend,
gossip, literary talk, i.e. appeals to vanity; (2) Art
(Renoir landscapes), the true escape into *Timelessness*;
(3) The office personality (Alibi Ike); (4) Old friends,
(relationships which date from before the Fall.)

Angoisse des Gares: A particularly violent form of
Angst. Bad when we meet someone at the station, but
worse when we are seeing them off; not present when
we are departing ourselves, but unbearable when
arriving in London, if only from a day in Brighton.
Since all Angst is identical, we may learn something
from these station-fears: Arrival-Angst is closely
connected with guilt, with the dread of something
terrible having happened during our absence. Death
of parents. Entry of bailiffs. Flight of loved one. Sensation worse at arriving in the evening than in the morning,
and much worse at Victoria and Waterloo than at
Paddington. This may have been due in my case to
my way of going abroad every vacation and therefore
returning to London with guilt-feelings about having

spent my money or not written to my parents, and to endless worry over work and debt.[1] Going to London as a schoolboy was a treat, as an undergraduate an ordeal, a surrender to justice. Later on the trips abroad grew longer, and returns were painful because of neglected household worries, and through a particularly strong guilt-feeling about not being at work, out-distanced by successful stay-at-home friends. But this is not all, for much of our anxiety is caused by horror of London itself; of the hideous entrails seen from the southern approaches, the high cost of living, the slums where we may die, embodiment of ugly and unnatural urban existence. When living in France, I began to have a similar feeling about Paris, though it has none of the same associations. I therefore deduce, that though it is wrong for us to live and work in great cities, to live away from them *without working* is worse. Angst begins at Reading, Woking or Croydon, or even in Paris, when we see the first grisly English faces home-ward bound at the Gare du Nord.

If, instead of Time's notorious and incompetent remedy, there was an operation by which we could be cured of loving, how many of us would not rush to have it!

To be kept for six months in a refrigerator or to hibernate in deep narcotic sleep, to be given new drugs, new glands, a new heart, and then to wake up with the memory swept clear of farewells and accusations, never more to be haunted by the grief-stricken eyes of our assassinated murderers!

But Angst descends; I wake up in anxiety; like a fog it overlays all my action, and my days are muffled with anguish. Somewhere in the mind are crossed the wires

[1] But why was I extravagant, why couldn't I write to them? —A deeper level of anxiety becomes apparent.

of fear and lust and all day long nature's burglar-alarm
shrills out in confusion. I dread the bell, the post, the
telephone, the sight of an acquaintance. Anguish,
anxiety, remorse and guilt: TOUT EST DÉGOÛT ET
MISÈRE. When even despair ceases to serve any creative
purpose, then surely we are justified in suicide. For
what better ground for self-destruction can there be
than to go on making the same series of false moves
which invariably lead to the same disaster, and to repeat
a pattern without knowing what it is or wherein
lies the flaw? And yet to perceive that in ourselves
there revolves a cycle of activity which is certain to
end in paralysis of the will, desertion, panic and despair
—always to go on loving those who have ceased to
love us, those who have quite lost all resemblance to
the beings whom once we loved! Suicide is catching:
what if the agony which self-murderers go through while
being driven to take their own lives, the conviction
that all is lost, be infectious also? And if you have
contracted it. Palinurus, if it has sought you out?

TE PALINURE PETENS, TIBI SOMNIA TRISTIA
PORTANS INSONTI?[1]

Madame du Deffand to Horace Walpole:
'Ennui. C'est une maladie de l'âme dont nous afflige
la nature en nous donnant l'existence; c'est le ver
solitaire qui absorbe tout . . . "Ah! je le répète sans
cesse, il n'y a qu'un malheur, celui d'être né."

Comment est-il possible qu'on craigne la fin d'une
vie aussi triste . . . Divertissez-vous, mon ami, le plus
que vous pourrez; ne vous affligez point de mon état,
nous étions presque perdus l'un pour l'autre; nous ne
nous devions jamais revoir; vous me regretterez, parce
qu'on est bien aise de se savoir aimé.'

[1] Looking for you, Palinurus, bringing you sad visions which
you have not deserved.

PART II

TE PALINURE PETENS

'YOU are very wise, very understanding and really very kindly. I wonder that you remain the critic. You can go beyond. You must have great fears and doubts, and you have overlaid another personality on the original one, a protective masked being which deals with what you imagine to be a harsh, cruel world.'—
HENRY MILLER to Palinurus.

'Had I followed my pleasure and chosen what I plainly have a decided talent for: police spy, I should have been much happier than I afterwards became.'—
KIERKEGAARD—*Journals*, 1843.

'Ne cherchez plus mon cœur; les bêtes l'ont mangé.'

APRIL MESSAGE

Pack up. Your situation is untenable, your loss irretrievable *y no hay remedio*. CHANGE YOUR BEDDING![1]

ORATE PRO NOBIS

Philip Heseltine, Harry Crosby, René Crevel, Mara Andrews.[2]

[1] Lamas do not die, but on reincarnation, are said to 'change their bedding.' 'And there is no remedy'. From a drawing of a dead man by Goya.

[2] Philip Heseltine (Peter Warlock) took his life by gas on 17th December 1930, aged thirty-six. The coroner read out part of

TE PALINURE PETENS

Spring in the Square, when the nile-green tendrils of the plane uncurl against the blue and·the Tree of Heaven prepares a book-plate entry; a soldier and his girl come in to kiss because the gate is open, it locks as they close it behind them and, hours later, they still wander round and round the empty garden like insects trying to escape from a pitcher plant. Lying on the fresh grass in the sun I read about opium as one would enquire about a new religion. Confessions of an opium-reader! Opium made de Quincey great and Cocteau serious. Would it prove the remedy, the 'Heart-balm'? To take a drug which exploded all the minefields of memory! And afterwards to come out not knowing who we are, not even being able to read and then to learn, and to discover some writers to whom we were strangely attracted,—as if we had known them in another life! And then as a fresh start to develop an Adult Personality, to attest that the one way to, be happy is to make other people happy; that virtue is social. 'Happiness lies in the approval of our fellow-men, unhappiness in their disapproval, to earn one is virtue, the other vice.' That is what I should teach, and if sometimes it sounded rather dull, that could only mean I was a little constipated.

---

a letter: 'I would very much rather visit you at some other time than Christmas. It is a season of the year which I dislike more and more as time goes on.'

Harry Crosby (according to Mr. Cowley in *Exile's Return*) planned his 'felo de se' on 31st October 1942, at the end of his fortieth year, by flying his plane till it crashed, 'a sun death into sun.' Unable to wait, he shot himself in New York in 1929.

René Crevel, surrealist poet, shot himself in Paris in 1935, aged thirty-four. He left a note: 'Je suis dégoûté de tout'.

Mara Andrews, once of the Ile Saint-Louis, committed suicide in New York while this was being written, aged thirty-two.

Civilization is an active deposit which is formed by the combustion of the Present with the Past. Neither in countries without a Present nor in those without a Past is it to be encountered. Proust in Venice, Matisse's birdcages overlooking the flower market at Nice, Gide on the seventeenth-century quais of Toulon, Lorca in Granada, Picasso by Saint-Germain-des-Prés: there lies civilization and for me it can exist only under those liberal regimes in which the Present is alive and therefore capable of assimilating the Past. Civilization is maintained by a very few people in a small number of places and we need only some bombs and a few prisons to blot it out altogether.

The civilized are those who get more out of life than the uncivilized, and for this we are not likely to be forgiven. One by one, the Golden Apples of the West are shaken from the tree.

The quince, coing, membrillo, marmelata, pyrus cydonia or portugalensis; emblem of love and happiness to the Ancients, was the golden fruit of the Hesperides and the love-apple which Greek maidens used to give their boys. It was also a Chinese symbol of long life and passion. I behold it in an emblem of the civilization of Europe with its hard flesh, bright colour and unearthly savour. The simple flower, the astringent fruit which ripens only in the south, the mysterious pips full of emulgent oil—all are significant. There are artists like quinces, 'of quaint and loose habit,' whose fragrance does not cloy.

Mysteries of nature: The properties of the quince, of the truffle (a truffle placed near a fresh egg will impregnate it with its odour), of the opium poppy and the peotl bud; the stormy life of wine; the cry of the cicada and the death's-head moth, the flight of the stag-beetle, the philoparasitism of the ant, the gaze of the mantis[1]; lemons and the scent of lemon-verbena and lemon-scented magnolia, the colour of gentians, the texture of water-lilies, the vegetable view of man. The smell of cigar-smoke, of coffee being roasted or of wine-barrels and of herbs in cooking is irresistible and demonstrates how intense and mutual is our collaboration.

Never would it occur to a child that a sheep, a pig, a cow or a chicken was good to eat, while, like Milton's *Adam*, he would eagerly make a meal off fruit, nuts, thyme, mint, peas and broad beans which penetrate further and stimulate not only the appetite but other vague and deep nostalgias. We are closer to the Vegetable Kingdom than we know; is it not for man alone that mint, thyme, sage, and rosemary exhale 'crush me and eat me!'—for us that opium poppy, coffee-berry, tea-plant and vine perfect themselves? Their aim is to be absorbed by us, even if it can only be achieved by attaching themselves to roast mutton.

'Les hommes et les insectes font partie de la même nature.'—CAILLOIS.

Why do ants alone have parasites whose intoxicating moistures they drink and for whom they will sacrifice even their young? Because as they are the most highly socialized of insects, so their lives are the most intolerable.

Protective colouring in insects represents not only their defence against the creatures who prey on them but their homage to the vegetables by whom they are guarded. The insect resembles a leaf at the wish of a tree. The vast vegetable world governs the tiny animal world by letting itself be assimilated.

[1] 'Elle épouse, elle tue et elle n'est que plus belle.'—(BINET on the Mantis.)

Why do sole and turbot borrow the colours and even the contours of the sea-bottom? Out of self-protection? No, out of self-disgust.

The civilization of the nineteenth century was founded on Coal, Electricity and Central Heating. These brought to the northern countries continuous industrial energy and a corresponding increase of population. With air-conditioning the civilization of the twentieth century can move south. This invention, by restoring their dynamic to the Mediterranean countries, may yet save Europe. We may even abolish the desert and the siesta as far south as Khartoum and Dakar, we may live to see the Mediterranean become as industrialized as the Great Lakes with Barcelona as Chicago and Athens as Detroit. England will appeal to these new and ventilated Carthaginians as a summer resort: a grey little fey little island.

The goal of every culture is to decay through over-civilization; the factors of decadence,—luxury, scepticism, weariness and superstition,—are constant. The civilization of one epoch becomes the manure of the next. Everything over-ripens in the same way. The disasters of the world are due to its inhabitants not being able to grow old simultaneously. There is always a raw and intolerant nation eager to destroy the tolerant and mellow. With the Brave New World we may hope to see whole populations on an equal footing, until all the nations wither in unison. We may say with Fontenelle 'Il faut du temps pour ruiner un monde, mais enfin, il ne faut que du temps.'

There was once a man (reputed to be the wisest in the world) who, although living to an untold age, confined his teaching to the one command: 'Endure!' At

length a rival arose who challenged him to a debate
which took place before a large assembly, 'You say
"Endure", cried his competitor, 'but I don't want to
endure. I wish to love and to be loved, to conquer and
create, I wish to know what is right, then do it and be
happy.' There was no reply from his opponent, and,
on looking more closely at the old creature, his adversary
found him to consist of an odd-shaped rock on which
had taken root a battered thorn that represented, by an
optical illusion, the impression of hair and a beard.
Triumphantly he pointed out the mistake to the authorities but they were not intimidated. 'Man or rock,' they
answered, 'does it really matter?' And at that moment
the wind, reverberating through the sage's moss-grown
orifice, repeated with a hollow sound: 'Endure!'

A love-affair can prosper only when both parties enter
free. If one lover is free and the other not, then in the
process of destroying their rival or the memory of their
rival, the one who is free will destroy the illusion of
their own virtue. A couple jointly possess so much of
their two selves that to hurt one is to wound the other,
and, even if they are wounded willingly, resentment is
set up. When we want a house we go to the house-
agent and inquire what is on the market; we do not
pick on the first one we like and force the tenant to
leave. The romantic prestige of adultery comes from
exaggerating the importance of chastity in the unmarried.
If fornication were no sin, then adultery would be
condemned, for it is a token form of murder. We do
not murder the rival husband or wife but we murder
their image in the eyes of those whom they love and
so prepare for the cancer of the ego and the slow death
by desertion. If our society allowed promiscuity only to
the free, that is to the unmarried or to those who had
both agreed on separation, and if it punished the breaking-

up of homes as it punishes robbery-with-violence, then the nervous breakdowns, the resort to alcohol and drugs, would disappear with much of the incurable unhappiness of the betrayed and forsaken.

The particular charm of marriage, which may grow irresistible to those who once have tasted it, is the duologue, the permanent conversation between two people who talk over everything and everyone till death breaks the record. It is this back-chat which, in the long run, makes a reciprocal equality more intoxicating than any form of servitude or domination. But for the artist it may prove dangerous; he is one of those who must look alone out of the window and for him to enter into the duologue, the non-stop performance of a lifetime, is a kind of exquisite dissipation which, despite the pleasure of a joint understanding of the human comedy, is likely to deprive him of those much rarer moments which are particularly his own. For this reason great artists are not always those who repose the most entire confidence in their wives (this is why second wives are sometimes best) and the relation of many an artist to his wife is apt to puzzle the spectator.

May 1st: Today we begin a new pincer movement against Angst, Melancholia and Memory's ever-festering wound: a sleeping-pill to pass the night and a Benzedrine to get through the day. The sleeping-pill produces a thick sleep, rich in dreams that are not so much dreams as tangible experiences, the Benzedrine a kind of gluttonous mental anger through which the sadness persists—O how sad,—but very much farther off. Whether they can ever combine in the mind to produce a new energy remains to be proven.

When I take Vitamin B, Metatone or other tonics, they render me calm, coarse and sensual; the voice becomes deeper, the manner more robust. Yet I am aware that this is not my real personality, but a toned-up film version, an escape from the serious ego, and soon I return to my true diffident and dyspeptic self. Confidence does not become me.

Ennui is the condition of not fulfilling our potentialities; remorse of not having fulfilled them; anxiety of not being able to fulfil them,—but what are they?

Let us take such a simple idea as the desire to improve, to become better. Is it a natural human instinct or is it the result of early conditioning? Crocodiles, king-crabs, eagles, do not evolve and yet they seem perfectly content with their humble status. And many human beings enjoy a quiet existence without feeling themselves obliged to expand or develop. With the desire to evolve arises the fear of remaining static, or guilt. If there were no parents to make us try to be good, no schoolmasters to persuade us to learn, no one who wished to be proud of us, would not we be happier? Promise is the white child's burden of which the savage, in his pre-mental bliss, has never heard. When we are sick we revert to our childhood patterns. Do we not live according to them in some degree when we are well? Heard, for example, is the son of a puritan clergyman, Huxley is by birth a public-spirited Victorian; what is their evolutionary zeal but a duty-reflex conditioned by their upbringing? Does Nature care in the least whether we evolve or not? Her instincts are for the gratification of hunger and sex, the destruction of rivals and the protection of offspring. What monster first slipped in the idea of progress? Who destroyed our conception of happiness with these growing-pains?

THE UNQUIET GRAVE

The triple decadence: Decadence of the material; of the writer's language. The virgin snow where Shakespeare and Montaigne used to cut their deep furrows, is now but a slope flattened by innumerable tracks until it is unable to receive an impression. Decadence of the myth, for there is no longer a unifying belief (as in Christianity or in Renaissance Man) to permit a writer a sense of awe and of awe which he shares with the mass of humanity. And even the last myth of all, the myth of the artist's vocation, of 'l'homme c'est rien, l'œuvre c'est tout', is destroyed by the times, by the third decadence, that of society. In our lifetime we have seen the arts advance further and further into an obscure and sterile cul-de-sac. Science has done little to help the artist, beyond contributing radio, linotype and the cinema; inventions which enormously extend his scope, but which commit him more than ever to the policy of the State and the demands of the ignorant. Disney is the tenth-rate Shakespeare of our age, forced by his universal audience to elaborate his new-world sentimentality with increasing slickness. There may arise Leonardos of the screen and microphone who will astound us but not until the other arts have declined into regional or luxury crafts, like book-binding, cabinet-making, thatching or pargetting. Today an artist must expect to write in water and to cast in sand.

Yet to live in a decadence need not make us despair; it is but one technical problem the more which a writer has to solve.

Even in the most socialized community, there must always be a few who best serve it by being kept isolated. The artist, like the mystic, naturalist, mathematician

54

or 'leader', makes his contribution out of his solitude. This solitude the State is now attempting to destroy, and a time may come when it will no more tolerate private inspiration. State Socialism in politics is bound to lead to social realism in the arts, until the position is reached that whatever the common man does not understand is treason. Yet it is a mistake completely to identify the State with a philistine father-figure and so to react blindly against it. For the State includes its own critics and their objections may lead to change. Today the State shows a benevolent face to Culture-Diffusion but to those who produce culture no trace of sympathy or indulgence, with the result that we are becoming a nation of commentators, of critics and hack-explainers, most of whom are ex-artists. Everything for the Milk-bar, nothing for the cow! Patiently and obstinately the artist must convince the State that, in the long run, it will be judged by its art and that, if the State is to replace the private patron, then it must imitate and even surpass that patron's tolerance, humility and liberality. When will the State say, 'Here is a thousand pounds, young man; go anywhere you like for six months, and bring me back something beautiful'?

A great artist is like a fig-tree whose roots run a hundred feet underground in search of tea-leaves, cinders and old boots. Art which is directly produced for the Community can never have the same withdrawn quality as that which is made out of the artist's solitude. For this possesses the integrity and bleak exhilaration that are to be gained only from the absence of an audience and from communion with the primal sources of unconscious life. One cannot serve both beauty and power: 'Le pouvoir est essentiellement stupide.' A public figure can never be an artist and no artist should ever become one unless, his work being done, he should choose to retire into public life.

An artist grows into a public figure through being always willing to address strangers. 'Pauvre et sans honneurs,' wrote Valéry of Mallarmé, 'la nudité de sa condition avilissait tous les avantages des autres . . . Tout leur semblait naïf et lâche après qu'ils l'avaient lu.'

A Chinese Parallel: Hui Tzu was prime minister in the Liang State. Chuang Tzu went thither to visit him.

Someone remarked: 'Chuang Tzu has come. He wants to be minister in your place.'

Thereupon Hui Tzu was afraid, and searched all over the State for three days and three nights to find him.

Then Chuang Tzu went to see Hui Tzu and said: 'In the south there is a bird. It is a kind of phœnix. Do you know it? It started from the south sea to fly to the north sea. Except on the wu-t'ung tree it would not alight. It would eat nothing but the fruit of the bamboo, drink nothing but the purest spring water. An owl which had got the rotten carcass of a rat looked up as the phœnix flew by, and screeched. Are you not screeching at me over your kingdom of Liang?' (*Musings of a Chinese Mystic.*)

May 4th: Failure of pincer movement. Am unwilling to take sleeping pills which are used up by my friends. Benzedrine has lost effect. Apathy, sluggishness and morning tears return with the sense of 'All-is-lost' and the torture of two faces.

> '. . . et me laissez enfin
> Dans ce petit coin sombre avec mon noir chagrin.'

What is the use of useless suffering? Where is the escape? What can one ever make out of the *nessun maggior dolore*, the stranglehold of the past, the heart broken but never dead? 'Je le répète sans cesse, il n'y a qu'un malheur, celui d'être né.'

Is it possible to love any human being without being torn limb from limb? No one was ever made wretched in a brothel; there need be nothing angst-forming about the sexual act. Yet a face seen in the tube can destroy our peace for the rest of the day, and once a mutual attraction develops it is too late; for when sexual emotion increases to passion, then something starts growing which possesses a life of its own and which, easily though it may be destroyed by ignorance and neglect, will die in agony and go on dying after it is dead.

As bees their sting, so the promiscuous leave behind them in each encounter something of themselves by which they are made to suffer.

It is the fear of middle-age in the young, and of old-age in the middle-aged, which is the prime cause of infidelity, that infallible rejuvenator.

When young we are faithful to individuals, older we grow more loyal to a situation or a type. Confronted by such specimens, we seem to know all about them in an instant (which is true) and thus in spite of our decreasing charm we sweep them off their feet, for young people do not understand themselves and, fortunately for us, can still be hypnotized by those who do.

The mind has its own womb to which, baffled by speculation, it longs to return; the womb of Homer and Herodotus, of the pastoral world where men and gods were ruled by the same passions and where all our personal problems seemed easy of solution. Then the womb fills with the Middle Ages, with the Popes, the Crusades

57

and the Renaissance. For some it stretches to include the court of Charles II, or the writers of the reign of Anne; it is the Hôtel des Grands Hommes, the Pantheon of mythical or historical figures who were masters of their surroundings, arbiters of their destiny and who went through life bundled together in a well-documented cats'-cradle of loving intimacy.

Desire to smoke opium comes back. 'It dulls the moral sense.'

> In blackest noon the shutter falls
> That folds me from the slanting day.
> Before the night a Stranger calls
> Who strikes the fearless and the gay.
>
> There is no love however deep
> Can stay the verdict in his eye,
> There is no laugh however sweet
> Can drown the moment's passing sigh.

'L'obésité a une influence fâcheuse sur les deux sexes, en ce qu'elle nuit à la force et à la beauté . . . L'obésité nuit à la beauté en détruisant l'harmonie de proportion primitivement établie.'

'Proposer à des obèses de se lever le matin, c'est leur percer le cœur.'—BRILLAT-SAVARIN.

Imprisoned in every fat man a thin one is wildly signalling to be let out.

A lazy person, whatever the talents with which he set out, will have condemned himself to second-hand thoughts and to second-rate friends.

Intense emotion, a mixture of relief and despair, at reading Sainte-Beuve's notebook *Mes Poisons*, and discovering 'This is me.' This Elegiac, as he styled himself, who quotes my favourite lines of Latin poetry and who sums up happiness as reading Tibullus in the country 'avec une femme qu'on aime,' who calls himself 'le dernier des délicats,' who loved, suffered and was disillusioned, and yet who recognizes love as the true source of happiness, who is sceptical of everyone and everything, a smaller man though a better artist than his romantic contemporaries; who loves the eighteenth century but was never taken in, who hated puritans and prigs and pedants but knew how the wine of remorse is trodden from the grapes of pleasure, and who, with all his scholarship and self-analysis, was at heart a Taoist, respecting the essential mystery ('le vrai c'est le secret de quelques-uns') and what he calls his 'âme pastorale',—how deeply moving to listen to such a voice from the past which in the present becomes an inspiration! I feel like a cringing cur kicked about in a crowd, which, running down an alley, finds there silence, an apprehension of revelation, and then, round a corner, comes suddenly upon a huge dark doggy statue, a canine colossus from another age; awe-inspiring and faith-restoring, lending him courage and wishing him well.

WISDOM OF SAINTE-BEUVE 1804–69

'L'épicuréisme bien compris est la fin de tout.'

'Que m'importe, pourvu que je fasse *quelque chose* le matin, et que je sois *quelque part* le soir.'

'La saturation, il y a un moment où cela vient dans ce repas qu'on appelle la vie: il ne faut qu'une goutte alors pour faire déborder la coupe du dégoût.'

.   .   .   .   .

'Il y a des moments où la vie, le fond de la vie se rouvre au dedans de nous comme une plaie qui saigne et ne veut pas se fermer.'

'Je suis resté avant tout un Elégiaque et un rêveur. Une grande et solide partie des jours, même aux années réputées graves, s'est passée pour moi dans les regrets stériles, dans les vagues désirs de l'attente, dans les mélancolies et les langueurs qui suivent le plaisir.'

'Je n'ai jamais conçu l'amour sans le mystère, et là où était le mystère, là pour moi déjà était l'amour.'

'Ne me demandez pas ce que j'aime et ce que je crois, n'allez pas au fond de mon âme.'

EPICTETUS: 'When God fails to provide for you, then He is giving the signal of retreat. He has opened the door and says to you, "Come"—'Where?—"To nothing fearful, but thither whence you were born, to things friendly and akin to you, the Elements".'

Illumination: Tout mon mal vient de Paris. Rue Delambre, Quai d'Anjou, Rue de Vaugirard. Aïe!
    'Ahi tu passasti, eterno sospiro mio.'

The hard black ball of suicidal despair. The door is open.
NERVAL: 'Arrivé sur la Place de la Concorde, ma pensée était de me détruire.'
Bad moment; the door is open, Paris 'ma plaie et ma fatalité.'

> 'The wind doth blow today my love
> And a few small drops of rain.'
>   .   .   .   .   .

TE PALINURE PETENS

As the lights in the penitentiary grow dim when the current is switched on for the electric chair, so we quiver in our hearts at a suicide, for there is no human life self-taken for which all society is not to blame.

WISDOM OF CHAMFORT (1741–1794)

'L'indécision, l'anxiété sont à l'esprit et à l'âme ce que la question est au corps.'

'Les passions font *vivre* l'homme; la sagesse le fait seulement *durer*.'

'Quand on a été bien tourmenté, bien fatigué par sa propre sensibilité, on s'aperçoit qu'il faut vivre au jour le jour, oublier beaucoup, enfin *éponger la vie* à mesure qu'elle s'écoule.'

'Otez l'amour-propre de l'amour, il en reste trop peu de chose . . . l'amour, tel qu'il existe dans la société, n'est que l'échange de deux fantaisies et le contact de deux épidermes.'

'Un homme amoureux qui plaint l'homme raisonnable me paraît ressembler à un homme qui lit des contes de fées, et qui raille ceux qui lisent l'histoire.'

'Presque tous les hommes sont esclaves, par la raison que les Spartiates donnaient de la servitude des Perses, faute de savoir prononcer la syllabe *non*. Savoir prononcer ce mot et savoir vivre seul sont les deux seuls moyens de conserver sa liberté et son caractére.'

In the jungles of South America grows a trumpet flower fourteen inches deep, and there too is found a moth with a proboscis of the same length, the one creature able to penetrate to the honey and so ensure the plant's

61

fertilization. I, Palinurus, am such an orchid, growing daily more untempting as I await the Visitor who never comes.

> 'On a pour ma personne une aversion grande
> et quelqu'un de ces jours il faut que je me pende.'

Yet there are many who dare not kill themselves for fear of what the neighbours will say.

In the small hours when the acrid stench of existence rises like sewer gas from everything created, the emptiness of life seems more terrible than its misery, 'Inferum deplorata silentia'...

Streets of Paris, pray for me; beaches in the sun, pray for me; ghosts of the lemurs, intercede for me; plane-tree and laurel-rose, shade me; summer rain on quays of Toulon, wash me away.

A young man who wished to marry consulted his uncle, an old courtier of the Prince of Wales' set. 'No one will want to marry you as you are,' said his uncle. 'You must get polish, your own particular aroma. Take a house, get to know about furniture and painting, buy the new books, listen to music, know whom to entertain and how to shake a dry Martini. Then you'll have something to offer and all the right mothers will snap you up.' The young man did as he was told and, some fifteen years later, he called again on the ancient week-ender of Fort Belvedere, whose old eyes now were seldom far from tears or alcohol.

'My house is perfect,' squeaked the brittle youth, 'the pictures are pure bliss, the bindings of green morocco catch the light of the evening sun; my *Louis Seize* commodes belly out in the alcoves, there are

62

Malvern water and biscuits by every bed and in each lavatory the toilet-paper, loosely arranged in scented sheets, is weighted down by a coloured stone. Ladies cry themselves into my life, then cough their way out of it; nobody who comes to luncheon remembers afterwards anything they have said. I am at last perfectly eligible. What shall I do?'

The old Beau laughed and lit his third cigar. 'Just carry on,' he chuckled; 'I think we've got *you* out of the wood'.

Bournemouth. Branksome Towers Hotel. Steamy tropical atmosphere, avenues of villas hidden in evergreens; the hotel with long vine-hung veranda and lawn sloping to the sea, dimly visible through a group of leaning pine-trees. The pines here with their undergrowth of rhododendron and arbutus form the northernmost tip of the maritime forest which stretches from Hossegor, near Bayonne, by the Landes and Royan, the Ile d'Oleron, La Rochelle, the Vendean coast, La Baule and the Landes of Brittany, to expire at Bournemouth and Le Touquet. Across the sea lies the unspoilt, uninhabited paradise of the Isle of Purbeck with its sandy beaches and chalk promontories.

Led by chance to discover the hanging foot-bridge over Alum Chine. Walking over the quivering planks I felt rooted, as in a nightmare, to the spot in the centre where the asphalt road lies directly underneath, a leaden water-snake uncurling through pine and giant hemlock. To drag one's sticky feet across was like plunging through a bog. What a place to make away with oneself or some loved one!

L'ennui de la campagne; l'angoisse des villes. Chaque fois que je rentre à Londres, j'assiste à un crime.

●　　●　　●　　●　　●

I am now forced to admit that anxiety is my true condition, occasionally intruded on by work, pleasure, melancholy or despair.

STEKEL: 'All neurotics are at heart religious. Their ideal is pleasure without guilt. The neurotic is a criminal without the courage to commit a crime . . . Every neurotic is an actor playing a particular scene. . . . Anxiety is repressed desire. Every individual who cannot find a form of sex-satisfaction adequate to himself suffers from an anxiety neurosis. . . . It is the disease of a bad conscience.'

A mistake which is commonly made about neurotics is to suppose that they are interesting. It is not interesting to be always unhappy, engrossed with oneself, malignant or ungrateful, and never quite in touch with reality. Neurotics are heartless: as Baudelaire wrote 'tout homme qui n'accepte pas les conditions de la vie vend son âme.'

The true index of a man's character is the health of his wife.

'Aimer et haïr, ce n'est qu'éprouver avec une passion singulière l'être d'un être.'

'Quand l'univers considère avec indifférence l'être que nous aimons, qui est dans la vérité?'—JOUHANDEAU.

We think we recognize someone in passing. A mistake, but a moment later we run into them. This pre-view was our arrival on their wavelength, within their magnetic orbit.

Like the glow-worm; dowdy, minute, passive, yet full of mystery to the poet and erotic significance to its fellows; so everything and everybody eternally radiate a dim light for those who care to seek. The strawberry hidden under the last leaf cries, 'Pick me'; the forgotten book, in the forgotten bookshop, screams to be discovered. The old house hidden in the hollow agitates itself violently at the approach of its pre-destined admirer. Dead authors cry 'Read me'; dead friends say 'Remember me'; dead ancestors whisper, 'Unearth me'; dead places, 'Revisit me'; and sympathetic spirits, living and dead, are continually trying to enter into communion. Physical or intellectual attraction between two people is a constant communication. Underneath the rational and voluntary world lies the involuntary, impulsive, integrated world, the world of Relation in which everything is one; where sympathy and antipathy are engrossed in their selective tug-of-war.

We learn a new word for the first time. Then it turns up within the next hour. Why? Because words are living organisms impelled by a crystallizing process to mysterious agglutinative matings at which the word-fancier is sometimes privileged to assist. The glow-worms light up. . . . The individual also is like a moving mirror or screen which reflects in its motion an ever-changing panorama of thoughts, sensations, faces and places, and yet the screen is always being guided to reflect one film rather than another, always seeking a chosen *querencia*. In the warm sea of experience we blob around like plankton, we love-absorb or hate-avoid each other or are avoided or are absorbed, devoured and devouring. Yet we are no more free than the cells in a plant or the microbes in a drop of water but are all held firmly in tension by the pull of the future and the tug of the past.

'Du moment que je me fus assuré de ce point que j'étais soumis aux épreuves de l'initiation sacrée, une

THE UNQUIET GRAVE

force invincible entra dans mon esprit. Je me jugeais un héros vivant sous le regard des dieux; tout dans la nature prenait des aspects nouveaux, et des voix secrétes sortaient de la plante, de l'arbre, des animaux, des plus humbles insectes, pour m'avertir et m'encourager. Le langage de mes compagnons avait des tours mystérieux dont je comprenais le sens, les objets sans forme et sans vie se prêtaient eux-mêmes aux calculs de mon esprit; des combinaisons de cailloux, des figures d'angles, de fentes ou d'ouvertures, des découpures de feuilles, des couleurs, des odeurs et des sons, je voyais ressortir des harmonies jusqu'alors inconnues. "Comment", me disais-je, "ai-je pu exister si longtemps hors de la nature et sans m'identifier à elle? Tout vit, tout agit, tout se correspond; les rayons magnétiques émanés de moi-même ou des autres traversent sans obstacle la chaîne infinie des choses créées; c'est un réseau transparent qui couvre le monde, et dont les fils déliés se communiquent de proche en proche aux planètes et aux étoiles." Captif en ce moment sur la terre, je m'entretiens avec le chœur des astres qui prend part à mes joies et à mes douleurs!'—G. DE NERVAL: *Aurélia*.[1]

In the break-up of religions and creeds there is but one deity whose worshippers have multiplied without a set-back. The Sun. In a few years there will be a stam-

[1] This piece, written by Nerval in his madness, resembles a late landscape of Van Gogh. The intense associations of atomical pantheism become what mental doctors call 'Delusions of Reference'. In manic elation communication seems to exist between inanimate objects and the Observer. Flowers signal to him, stones cry out, and all nature approves. In suicidal depression the same phenomena arise, but in this case nature seems to pass a vote of censure; inanimate objects urge the Observer to make a thorough good job of it. Are both fatigue and ecstasy poisons which distort our relation to external reality? Or do they liberate deep-buried instinctive perceptions of relationship to which normally we are blind?

66

pede towards this supreme anæsthetic. Scotland will pour itself into Southern England, Canada into the U.S.A., the U.S.A, dwindle to Florida, California and New Mexico, while Southern Englanders will have migrated en masse to the Mediterranean. The temperate zone, especially for women, is becoming uninhabitable. Let us leave England to retired Generals and culture-diffusionists, goose-fleshed politicians and bureaucrats, while the rest of us heliotropes cluster nearer to the great bronze disk of church-emptying Apollo, hardener of heart and skin.

July: Once more the bold Dragonfly of pleasure has brushed me with its wing. Divine Sainte-Beuve,— 'L'épicuréisme bien compris',—and Hume, the Northern Epicurus. Late June, July and early August— fruit-eating months when the English become callous, pleasure-ridden, amorous and Elizabethan. It is necessary.

After the long suicidal winter Pleasure comes to rescue us from the desert island of the ego and allow us two months' grace. Good-bye sick Pascal and his mouldy troupe; gaunt Kierkegaard, hunch-backed Leopardi, wheezing Proust and limping Epictetus with his Open Door! Midsummer greeting to La Fontaine, Congreve, Aristippus, Horace and Voltaire! Good-bye morning tears, 'All-is-lost', never-again, doubt, despair! Welcome cheese-breathing hang-over, tipsy mornings for gargling poetry, asparagus afternoons, gull's-egg evenings, affection slopping over into gossip, who-was-there and ring-a-ling! Taoism at last rewarded! 'Flower o' the Quince', . . . Hour of the Broad Bean.

If all the world loved pleasure as much as Palinurus there would be no war.

THE UNQUIET GRAVE

THE PLAY-BOY PERMIT

I

'Le plaisir crée une franc-maçonnerie charmante. Ceux qui y sont profès se reconnaissent d'un clin d'œil, s'entendent sans avoir besoin de paroles, et il se passe là de ces choses imprévues, sans prélude et sans suites, de ces hasards de rencontre et de mystère qui échappent au récit, mais qui remplissent l'imagination et qui sont un des enchantements de la vie. Ceux qui y ont goûté n'en veulent plus d'autres.'—SAINTE-BEUVE.

II

'Les hommes trouveront toujours que la chose la plus sérieuse de leur existence, c'est jouir.'—FLAUBERT.

Dining-out is a vice, a dissipation of spirit punished by remorse. We eat, drink and talk a little too much, abuse all our friends, belch out our literary preferences and are egged on by accomplices in the audience to acts of mental exhibitionism. Such evenings cannot fail to diminish those who take part in them. They end on Monkey Hill.

Society: A perfect dinner-party for sixteen. Each person as carefully chosen as an instrument in an orchestra,—yet how many of the guests would rather be engaged that evening in tête-à-tête? Or be glad to leave early for a brothel?

MESSAGE FROM THE ID

'If you would collect women instead of books, I think I could help you.'

'And there came thunder and lightning and pestilence and famine and the people were sore afraid. And the
68

Lord spake out of the tempest and out of the whirl-wind and the earth quaked and all the people trembled with fear, and the Lord cried with a mighty voice: "When thou goest away for weekends thou shalt not stay over Monday; over thy luncheon not long shalt thou squat, nor shalt thou take taxis, nor buy books; third class thou shalt travel, not first; neither shalt thou drink wine nor giggle nor spoon; but thou shalt sorrow and sweat wherever thou goest,—for I the Lord thy God am a jealous God and behold I will crush thee as a slimy worm." And lo, there fell a silence over the earth and the land lay barren a thousand years.'

Anxiety again, *en grande tenue*. The two faces. Every-thing connected with them is excruciating: people, places, sounds, smells, habits. An old letter coils up and explodes like a land-mine, an inscription in a book pronounces a life-sentence, gramophone records screech from the grave; even the harmless sunbeam and the green surge of summer out of doors are decoys which ambush the heart at a sultry corner. *Da dextram misero!* O, never to have met or never to have parted! Living in the present (the one escape) can only be contrived by drugs, by an injection of work or pleasure or by the giving 'which plays you least false'. The past is a festering wound; the present the compress vainly applied, painfully torn off. Paris, Chelsea, Cannes—*misère!* We are all serving a life-sentence in the dungeon of self.

Sainte-Beuve's poem, 'Dans l'île Saint-Louis'. He knew.

Imagination=nostalgia for the past, the absent; it is the liquid solution in which art develops the snapshots of reality. The artist secretes nostalgia round life, as a worm plasters its tunnel, a caterpillar spins a cocoon

69

or as a sea-swallow masticates her nest. Art without imagination is as life without hope.

Egotism sucks us down like the law of gravity. In the small hours this law is somewhat weakened, we are less subject to it and even the self-centredness with which the earth rotates on its axis, seems to fade. As egotism subsides we grow more conscious of the meagre foundation of our lives, of the true nature of the Authorities whom we try to please and by whom we wish to be loved—those who feed our lost selves with their admiration.

For a dark play-girl in a night-club I have pined away, for a dead school boy, for a bright angel-vixen I have wept in vain. If this thoughtless woman were to die there would be nothing to live for, if this faithless girl forgot me there would be no one for whom to write. These two unseen and otherwise occupied figures compose the fragile arch of my being and constitute a Tribunal which they have long ceased to attend.

Miserable Orpheus who, turning to lose his Eurydice, beholds her for the first time as well as the last.

'The self-torments of melancholiacs, which are without doubt pleasurable, signify a gratification of sadistic tendencies and of hate, both of which relate to an object and in this way have both been turned round upon the self. In the end the sufferers usually succeed in taking revenge, by the circuitous path of self-punishment, on the original object who occasioned the injury and who is usually to be found in their near neighbourhood. No neurotic harbours thoughts of suicide which are not murderous impulses against others redirected upon himself.'—FREUD.

70

The cycle of the hours. 'The Lars and Lemures moan with midnight plaint.' 1 a.m.: Anger turns to Misery. 2 a.m.: Misery to Panic. The low tide and nadir of hope about 2 a.m. to 4. Magical Euphoria wells from 4 a.m. to 6—the thalamic 'All Clear'; Peace and Certainty arrive through Despair. All morning the tide of confidence rolls in with high water of egotism from 2 p.m. to 3. (We are farthest then from the idea of death as in the nocturnal small hours we are nearest.) Momentary depression at sunset, though often at my best from 6 o'clock to 10. Then the bilges begin to empty.

Thought can be made to take liberties by artificial stimulation of the brain. The cortex is a machine for thinking. It can be 'revved up', slowed down, choked, fed various types of fuel according to the ideas it is required to produce. When the mixture is too rich, as in the small hours, the engine pinks, whence the manic symptom, 'Flight of Ideas'.

Thus tea, coffee, alcohol stimulate.

So do heights, wet days, south-west gales, hotel bedrooms in Paris and windows overlooking harbours. Also snow, frost, the electric bell outside a cinema at night, sex-life and fever.

Cigars, tisanes, long draughts of water and fruit-juice have a clearing, calming effect. They 'rev' down the motor and overcome stoppages. And so do sitting still, relaxing climates, luxury, constipation, music, sun-bathing, hang-overs, listening to fountains, waves and waterfalls.

A thorough knowledge of opium, benzedrine, phosphorus and other drugs should make it possible for us to feed the brain the right mixture according to the effect desired; whether we contemplate a work of the imagination (putting ideas into our heads) or of the intellect (analysis, reasoning, memory).

When we decide to write, we should first consider the ingredients involved. Proportions of heart and head, of judgement and imagination. 'A peach of an essay', 'a melon of a poem', 'a quince of a book',—we must let ourselves be impregnated by an archetypal form. Then we should treat the personality with the right mixture till the glaze (style) is suitable,—'for my philosophical novel with a milligramme of nostalgia, I am taking ephedrine twice a week, opium once— with a little mescaline to loosen up my imagery and a massage on the nape of the neck to stimulate the thalamus after the monthly orgy. I am writing two-thirds standing up in the early morning, one-third in the afternoon lying down. My supervisor is a Jungian.'

Last Words on Opium-Reading

'L'opium est la seule substance végétale qui nous communique l'état végétal. Par lui nous avons une idée de cette autre vitesse des plantes.'

'L'opium apprivoisé adoucira le mal des villes.'— COCTEAU.

'Here were the hopes which blossom in the paths of life reconciled with the peace which is in the grave.'— DE QUINCEY.

Others merely live; I vegetate.

O sacred solitary empty mornings, tranquil meditation— fruit of book-case and clock-tick, of note-book and arm-chair; golden and rewarding silence, influence of sun-dappled plane-trees, far-off noises of birds and horses, possession beyond price of a few cubic feet of air and an hour of leisure! This vacuum of peace is the state from which art should proceed, for art is made by the alone for the alone, and now this cerulean atmosphere, which we should all be able to take for granted, has become an unattainable end.

The reward of art is not fame or success but intoxication: that is why so many bad artists are unable to give it up.

What fathers would I like to vindicate? Who, on reading Palinurus in the Asphodel Club will say, 'I told you so'? Aristippus, Horace, Tibullus, Montaigne, Saint Flaubert and Sainte-Beuve. But Pascal? He frightens me,— and Chamfort? I don't think so.

I have much more in common with Chamfort than with Pascal; sometimes I feel that I was Chamfort, for there is nothing of his that I might not, with luck, have written, yet it is by reading the thoughts of Pascal, (which I never could have written,) that I change and grow. Literary charm, arising out of the desire to please, excludes those flights of intellectual power which are more rewarding than pleasure.

The Predicament of Chamfort, 1741–94

His mother was a 'dame de compagnie', his father unknown, and he was christened merely 'Nicolas'. Mother and son came from Auvergne to Paris where Nicolas was a brilliant schoolboy. After dallying with the Church, he plunged into the world of letters. A love-child, Chamfort was swept to success by the favours of women, a success which exhausted him physically and led to serious disorders; however, he obtained a well-paid sinecure, a literary prize, and a stage triumph through his wit, his gallantry, and the love of his friends, until at forty he retired to Boileau's old home at Auteuil; there he fell in love with a 'dame de compagnie' to the

Duchesse de Maine, aged forty-eight, who died six months later. After her loss, he returned to Paris to become the cynical jester and licensed darling of the Court. 'My sentiments are republican, yet I live with courtiers. I love poverty, my friends are all rich; I believe that illusions are a necessary luxury of life, yet I live without any; I believe that passions are more useful to us than reason, yet I have destroyed my capacity for feeling.' When the Revolution broke out, Chamfort, a genuine republican, sided with his friend and admirer Mirabeau. He spoke at street corners and was one of the first to enter the Bastille. Though he lost all his pensions he plunged with enthusiasm into politics and contributed such slogans as 'Guerre aux châteaux, Paix aux chaumières'! and 'Moi, tout; le reste rien! Voilà le despotisme. Moi, c'est un autre; un autre c'est moi: voilà la démocratie'. In spite of a warning that his sallies would not be tolerated as indulgently as under the old regime, he soon began to mimic and satirize the new personages of the Revolution. In 1793 he sealed his fate with his description of Jacobin ethics: 'Sois mon frère ou je te tue'. 'I am not afraid,' he said, 'Je n'ai pas peur; n'ai-je pas toujours marché au premier rang de la phalange républicaine?' Denounced anonymously, he was taken to prison. He was released but almost immediately rearrested. Rather than lose his liberty at the hands of the Party to which he was convinced he belonged, he made an excuse to leave the room, and shot himself. The bullet broke his nose and went into his eye. He next tried to cut his throat with a razor. He partially recovered from his wounds but died soon afterwards from pneumonia. His last words were: 'Je m'en vais enfin de ce monde, où il faut que le cœur se brise ou se bronze'.

The complexity of Chamfort's character would seem to be due to his temperament as a love-child; he transmuted his passionate love for his mother into a general desire for affection which he concentrated at last on the elderly lady-in-waiting who resembled her. With this need for love went that equally violent feeling, so familiar to bastards, of a grievance against society. The warmth of his affections combined with his sense of injustice and his clear mind to propel him to the crest of the Revolution, but he was one of those observers who cannot blind themselves to the defects of men who logically carry out an ideal in action. Though he himself believed in their cause, he was a philosopher without hope and without pity.[1] Physically Chamfort was tall and handsome, an Adonis in youth, pale and exhausted in later life; he was a man who lived in spurts, and who seemed kept alive by the fire of his intelligence. Mirabeau called him 'noble et digne' and admired his 'tête électrique', Chateaubriand praised his cold blue eye. His predicament is one with which we are all familiar and there is every danger that it will soon become only too common; that of the revolutionary whose manners and way of life are attached to the old régime, whose ideals and loyalties belong to the new, and who, by a kind of courageous exhibitionism, is impelled to tell the truth about both, and to expect from the commissars of King Stork the applause for his sallies which they received from the courtiers of King Log. Most lovable of Chamfort's sayings which, remarkable though they be for splenetic violence, are apt to grow irritating through an excess of point, a somewhat vulgar urbanity, is his final outburst, just after he had attempted his life. He is speaking to a friend in his usual quiet tone

---

[1] 'All literature might be ransacked in vain for a more repulsive saying than this (of Chamfort): "A man must swallow a toad every morning if he wishes to be sure of finding nothing still more disgusting before the day is over".'—MORLEY: *Studies of Literature*, p. 95.

of familiar irony: 'Que voulez-vous? Voilà ce que c'est que d'être maladroit de la main: on ne réussit à rien, pas même à se tuer.' He began to explain how, instead of blowing out his brains, he had punctured his eye and the lower part of his forehead, then, instead of cutting his throat, he had gashed his neck and even hacked his chest without succeeding in stabbing his heart. 'Enfin,' he concludes, 'je me suis souvenu de Sénèque, et, en l'honneur de Sénèque, j'ai voulu m'ouvrir les veines; mais il était riche, lui; il avait tout à souhait, un bain bien chaud, enfin toutes ses aises; moi, je suis un pauvre diable, je n'ai rien de tout cela. Je me suis fait un mal horrible, et me voilà encore; mais j'ai la balle dans la tête, c'est là le principal. Un peu plus tôt, un peu plus tard, voilà tout.'

WISDOM OF CHAMFORT II

C'est un grand malheur de perdre, par notre caractère, les droits que nos talents nous donnent sur la société.

Il y a une certaine énergie ardente, mère ou compagne nécessaire de telle espèce de talents, laquelle pour l'ordinaire condamne ceux qui les possèdent au malheur. C'est une âpreté dévorante dont ils ne sont pas maîtres et qui les rend très-odieux.

En renonçant au monde et à la fortune, j'ai trouvé le bonheur, le calme, la santé, même la richesse; et, en dépit du proverbe, je m'aperçois que 'qui quitte la partie la gagne'.

La vie contemplative est souvent misérable. Il faut agir davantage, penser moins, et ne pas se regarder vivre.

Il faut recommencer la société humaine.

· · · · ·

TE PALINURE PETENS

Les fléaux physiques et las calamités de la nature humaine ont rendu la société nécessaire. La société a ajouté aux malheurs de la nature. Les inconvénients de la société ont amené la nécessité du gouvernement, et le gouvernement ajoute aux malheurs de la société. Voilà l'histoire de la nature humaine.

Les pauvres sont les nègres de l'Europe.

Quand un homme et une femme ont l'un pour l'autre une passion violente, il me semble toujours que . . . les deux amants sont l'un à l'autre *de par la nature*, qu'ils s'appartiennent *de droit divin*.

'Les prétentions sont une source de peines, et l'époque du bonheur de la vie commence au moment où elles finissent.'

'La pensée console de tout.'

When I turn to see what Sainte-Beuve thinks of Chamfort, how the old love will greet the new, I find him somewhat severe, the Superego judging the Ego. One would have expected him to feel more sympathy for a man so melancholy and disillusioned, one to whom, like himself, people were 'as those insects whose transparent tissue lets us see the veins and all the different shades of the blood'; instead he is over-critical, and a little alarmed by him. He admits that Chamfort's aphorisms are like 'des flèches acérées qui arrivent brusquement et sifflent encore', but he reapproaches him with being a bachelor and therefore a recluse on whom Nature took her revenge. With equivocal serenity this other bachelor, the dubious monk of letters of the Rue de Montparnasse, finds fault with Chamfort for two of his maxims—'Je ne veux point me marier, dans la crainte d'avoir un fils qui me ressemble', and 'Quiconque n'est pas misanthrope à quarante ans n'a jamais aimé les hommes'.

Unwillingly one has to admit the justice of Sainte-Beuve's profound, stern, yet not unsympathetic analysis. Compared to him, Chamfort is a Byronic adolescent. 'J'ai du Tacite dans la tête et du Tibulle dans le cœur,' writes Chamfort. 'Ni le Tibulle ni le Tacite,' cracks Sainte-Beuve, 'n'ont pu en sortir pour la postérité'. What makes Sainte-Beuve superior? He detected Chamfort's tragedy: that he was a moralist whose credentials have never quite been accepted, that there was too much egotism in his judgement (which reflects the guilty self-hatred of those who know that they are neglecting their talent through indolence and hedonism). Chamfort detested humanity, but, unlike Sainte-Beuve, he could find no compensation in the love of nature. Chamfort was a classical pagan, Sainte-Beuve a double-minded critic who had passed through the mystical experience and the Romantic Movement to a scepticism infinitely enriched by both.

Another view: 'I believe only in French culture, and I regard everything else in Europe which calls itself culture as a misunderstanding. . . . When one reads Montaigne, La Rochefoucauld, Vauvenargues and Chamfort, one is nearer to antiquity than with any group of authors in any other nation.'—NIETZSCHE.

And with Baudelaire, Flaubert, Sainte-Beuve, nearer to ourselves.

Those who are consumed with curiosity about other people but who do not love them should write maxims, for no one can become a novelist unless he love his fellow-men. Being myself contaminated by oriental philosophy, I cannot take people seriously, (Sabba dukka! 'In those countries human life is but a weed.') They all seem replaceable except for the few who carry away sections of ourselves which cannot be replaced. Once we believe that the ego is like a cell which by over-assertion of itself causes cancer, the cancer of developing at the expense of society or at the expense of the self's natural harmony with the order of things, a harmony which it drowns by its own din, then we can only dislike the pushing, confident extroverts who, with their petty ambitions, form the backbone of fiction. If we have no appetite for the idiosyncrasies of minor personalities, then we must fight shy of the novel which will end by seeming as grotesque to us as the portrait of an alderman to a Tibetan Lama.

> 'When the bells justle in the tower
> The hollow night amid,
> Then on my tongue the taste is sour
> Of all I ever did.'[1]

Vanished symptoms of health: early rising, early shaving, briskness in lavatory and bath, alacrity in crossing the street, care for personal appearance, horror of possessions, indifference to the newspaper, kindness to strangers, *Folie des Maures.*

August 7th: the first autumn day. For once I have lived in the present! Walked to the book-shop at closing time. Raining. A girl tried to get into the shop but the doors were bolted. Went out and followed her past the Zwemmer Gallery and through the streets towards St. Giles', only to lose her by the Cambridge Theatre, cursing the upbringing which has left me after all these

---

[1] Stanza dreamt by Professor Housman.

years unable to address a stranger. Much disturbed by the incident, for this girl, with her high forehead, pointed nose, full lips and fine eyes, her dark hair and her unhappy and sullen expression, personified both intelligence and beauty in distress. She was bare-legged and wore sandals, a green corduroy suit under a linen coat. With a feeling of intolerable frustration I watched her out of sight: 'o toi que j'eusse aimée'.

From my violent reaction to this encounter I was able to learn a little more about the nature of my emotions.

I. To fall in love at first sight there has to be what Sainte-Beuve called '*le mystère*'. In my case the mystery must take the form of a rejection of the industrial system and of the twentieth century. It is an aloofness, a suggestion of the primitive that I crave. Hence the appeal of sandals, which alone permit human beings to hold themselves naturally. This air of aloofness is incompatible with happiness since it springs from a feeling of isolation, a sense of rebellion and hostility towards society which cannot in these days make for contentment. Indeed, I think that women, when they achieve domestic happiness at the price of independence, forfeit most of their appeal.

II. This primitive and untamed expression is not enough; it must be illuminated by an interest in the arts, especially in modern painting and surrealism. The gipsy-look must correspond to the chaos of our time, to the spiritual wilderness of modern art. This taste is shared, I believe, by others who have made their peace with society. We are captivated by the feminine shadow of the self we might have been; in my case by that counterpart of the romantic writer who should have had the courage to reject society and to accept poverty for the sake of the development of his true personality. Now when I see such beings I hope that I can somehow be freed from my shortcomings by union with them. Hence the recurrent longing to forsake external reality for a dream and to plunge into a ritual flight.

Some fall in love with women who are rich, aristocratic or stupid. I am attracted by those who mysteriously hold out a promise of the integrity which I have lost; unsubdued daughters of Isis, beautiful as night, tumultuous as the moon-stirred Atlantic.[1]

III. Recognition takes place at the turn of the year and must be followed at once by the ritual flight and consummation in a cave.

To banish the rainy evening, the dripping plane-trees, the depression of Fitzroy Square and Charlotte Street and the afternoon's disappointment, I asked some friends round to drink a bottle of rum. Since old friends are almost indistinguishable from enemies, we talked about each other's vices. One said the vice of Palinurus was inconstancy. But is it not rather constancy? Fidelity to the experience of abandoning all the world for a new face with an invitation to ecstasy? Or is it that but one more autumn ruse for self-destruction?

'Shall I believe the *Syren* South again
And, oft-betray'd, not know the Monster Main?'

---

[1] Isis was represented as the moon rising from the sea: 'ista luce feminea collustrans cuncta moenia et udis ignibus nutriens laeta semina.—APULEIUS. MET.XI. [With her feminine light sharply bringing out the city walls, and with her damp fires nourishing the happy seed.]

PART III

LA CLE DES CHANTS

ILLUMINATION: 'La mélancolie elle-même n'est qu'un souvenir qui s'ignore.'—FLAUBERT.

The Sun warms out old memories, the Mist exhumes others, as they intensify the fragrance of trees or the smell of ferns.

First faint impression of urban autumn. There are memories which are brought into play by certain sounds, smells or changes in temperature; like those tunes which recur in the mind at a given time of year. With the sweeping up of the dead leaves in the square, the first misty morning, the first yellowing of the planes, I remember Paris and the old excitement of looking for autumn lodgings in an hotel. Streets round the Rue de l'Université, Rue Jacob, Rue de Bourgogne and Rue de Beaune, with their hotel signs and hall-ways where the concierge sits walled in by steamer trunks. A stuffy salon full of novels by Edith Wharton, the purple wall-paper which we will grow to hate as we lie in bed with grippe, the chintz screen round the bidet, the tall grey panelling with a cupboard four inches deep. . . .

Hôtel de l'Université for American college girls, Hôtel de Londres with a chestnut tree in the courtyard, Hôtel Jacob for wasting much time; Hôtel de Savoie, Hôtel Delambre, Hôtel de la Louisiane; central-heated
82

LA CLE DES CHANTS

Stations of the Cross: names that stir the lees within me.

For an angora pullover, for a red scarf, for a beret and some brown shoes I am bleeding to death; my heart is dry as a kidney.

Peeling off the kilometres to the tune of 'Blue Skies', sizzling down the long black liquid reaches of Nationale Sept, the plane trees going sha-sha-sha through the open window, the windscreen yellowing with crushed midges, she with the Michelin beside me, a handkerchief binding her hair . . .

'Le cœur a ses raisons',—and so have rheumatism and 'flu. The sole of the foot, the nape of the neck still recollect the embrace of the Mediterranean—pale water streaked with sapphirine sea-shadow, translucent under the Esterel.

Paris afternoons; the quiet of hotel bedroom and of empty lounge; the bed covered with clothes and magazines, the *Chicago Tribune*, the *Crapouillot*, the *Semaine à Paris*; programmes of the Pagoda Cinema, The Ursulines, Studio Vingt-huit; faraway cries of 'voici *l'Intran*' answered by the honking of horns . . .

Early morning on the Mediterranean: bright air resinous with Aleppo pine, water spraying over the gleaming tarmac of the Route Nationale and darkly reflecting the spring-summer green of the planes; swifts wheeling round the oleander, waiters unpiling the wicker chairs and scrubbing the café tables; armfuls of carnation on the flower-stall, pyramids of lemon and aubergine, *rascasses* on the fishmonger's slab goggling among the wine-dark urchins; smell of brioches from the bakers, sound of reed curtains jingling in the barber shop, clang of the tin kiosk opening for *Le Petit Var*. Our rope-soles warm up on the cobbles by the harbour

83

where the *Jean d'Agrève* prepares for a trip to the Islands and the Annamese boy scrubs her brass. Now cooks from many yachts step ashore with their market-baskets, one-eyed cats scrounge among the fish-heads, while the hot sun refracts the dancing sea-glitter on the café awning, until the sea becomes a green gin-fizz of stillness in whose depth a quiver of sprats charges and counter-charges in the pleasure of fishes.

Dead leaves, coffee grounds, grenadine, tabac Maryland, mental expectation,—perfumes of the Nord-Sud; autumn arrival at Pigalle or the sortie from Notre-Dame-des-Champs into the lights of Montparnasse where the chestnuts, glowing red by the métro entrance, live in a warmer climate than their fellows . . .

Our memories are card-indexes consulted and then returned in disorder by authorities whom we do not control.

Back-streets of Cannes; tuberoses in the window, the book-shop over the railway bridge which we comb for memoirs and detective stories while the cushions of the car deflate in the afternoon sun. *Petit Marseillais. Eclaireur de Nice:* head-lines about the Spanish war soaked in sun-bathing oil, torn maps, the wet bathing-dress wrapped in a towel,—and now we bring home memoirs, detective stories, tuberoses, round the danger-ous corner of the Rue d'Antibes and along the road by the milky evening sea.

The boredom of Sunday afternoon, which drove de Quincey to smoke opium, also gave birth to surrealism: hours propitious for making bombs.

August 15th: Wet Sunday recalling many others. 'Fantômes de Trouville', 'Sea-scape with frieze of girls.'

LA CLE DES CHANTS

Beaches of the West: Houlgate, Royan, Saint-Jean-de-Luz. A red digue, colour of porphyry. In the shops hang buckets, toy yachts, shrimping-nets and string-bags enclosing rubber balls with a dull bloom, of the same porphyry colour. Children in the shop are choosing their sandals and gym-shoes, girls are walking arm-in-arm along the promenade; the west wind from the sea spatters the jetty; old bills of casino galas with their faded 'Attractions' roll flapping among the tamarisks. Prowling from the Marquise de Sévigné tea room to the Potinière bar, dark and smelling of gin, we lie in wait for one more glimpse of the sea-side girls in their impregnable adolescence—before the Atlantic sun fades angrily over enormous sands, coloured like the under-belly of soles.

Saint-Jean-de-Luz. Buying a melon in the morning market and eating it for breakfast in a café on the Bidassoa; pursuing a macintosh, a beret and a strand of wet curls round the sea-wall in the rain. Maize and pimento, light-footed Basques with round lean faces dancing Fandango and Arin-Arin, playing pelota against the church wall while a huge green sunset agonizes through plate-glass windows. Angoisse des digues. . . .

Hemingway is great in that alone of living writers he has saturated his work with the memory of physical pleasure, with sunshine and salt water, with food, wine and making love and the remorse which is the shadow of that sun.

August 30th: Morning tears return; spirits at their lowest ebb. Approaching forty, sense of total failure: not a writer but a ham actor whose performance is clotted with egotism; dust and ashes; 'brilliant',—that is, not worth doing. Never will I make that extra effort to live according to reality which alone makes

85

good writing possible: hence the manic-depressiveness of my style,—which is either bright, cruel and superficial; or pessimistic; moth-eaten with self-pity.

Everything I have written seems to date except the last lines I set down. These appear quite different, absolute exceptions to the law—and yet what dates in them does not vary but remains the same—a kind of auto-intoxication which is brought out by the act of writing.

Approaching forty, I am about to heave my carcass of vanity, boredom, guilt and remorse into another decade.

> Lusisti satis, edisti satis, atque bibisti[1]
> Tempus abire tibi est.

Both my happiness and unhappiness I owe to the love of pleasure; of sex, travel, reading, conversation (hearing oneself talk), food, drink, cigars and lying in warm water.

Reality is what remains when these pleasures, together with hope for the future, regret for the past, vanity of the present, and all that composes the aroma of the self are pumped out of the air-bubble in which I shelter.

When we have ceased to love the stench of the human animal, either in others or in ourselves, then are we condemned to misery, and clear thinking can begin. 'Le seule réalité, c'est le souci (*sorge*) dans toute l' échelle des êtres. Pour l'homme perdu dans le monde et ses divertissements, ce souci est une peur brève et fuyante. Mais que cette peur prenne conscience d'elle-même et elle devient l'angoisse (*angst*), climat perpetuel de l'homme lucide "dans lequel existence se retrouve."'
—HEIDEGGER.

[1] You have played enough, you have eaten and drunk enough. It's time you went home.'—HORACE.

O, qu'elle est belle l'étoile de mer! The starfish sprawling on an Atlantic beach streaked with shallow pools; ridges of mackerel sand taut under the bare foot; the sun on the spilt water-beads which mark the tide by streamers of bladder-wrack and melting jelly-fish; all these will return and the leisure to enjoy them, to paddle under a razor-shell sky among rocks where the transparent prawn leans up against the weed like an old man reading in a public library, feathering with his legs and feelers and rocketing backwards with a flick of the tail. And there will be time to observe the blenny where it lies half out of the water, the hermit-crab and anemone, the pin-pointed urchin, the sea-slug on her green sea-salad, the swaying zoster.

> O litus vita mihi dulcius, O mare! felix[1]
> qui licet ad terras ire subinde meas!

Midnight harbours of France, O rain-swept lights on the quay!

Approaching forty, a singular dream in which I almost grasped the meaning and understood the nature of what it is that wastes in wasted time.

Present pleasure kills time, it is like sleep, a harmless anæsthetic: harmless when once we have recognized that our life is so painful as to need what otherwise would distil both guilt and remorse. If, however, we understand that the love of pleasure can be increased or decreased according to need, then as the pleasure fades into the past it will leave behind only a sense of nostalgia and this nostalgia can be converted into art, and, once so converted, all trace of guilt is washed away.

Art is memory: memory is re-enacted desire.

[1] O sea shore sweeter to me than life, O sea, happy am I who may come at last to go to my own lands.—PETRONIUS.

The body remembers pleasure past and on being made aware of it, floods the mind with sweetness. Thus the smell of sun-warmed pine-needles and the bloom on ripe whortle-berries reopen the file marked Kitzbühel and bring back the lake with its muddy water, raft conversations and pink water-lilies; the drive over the white Alpine road through the black fir-wood or the walk over the meadow where runnels of water sing in wooden troughs beside the châlets. Remembering all this communicates several varieties of pleasure; those which, like lying in a thick peat-bath on a rainy evening, are purely sensual, which are social like playing bridge in the afternoon or intellectual like talking to Pierre; pleasures of vanity like flirting in the Tiefenbrünner or buying local jackets and *lederhosen*,—and ever present, as the bald peak of the Kitzbühlerhorn, the unpunished delights of health; of mountain air, good food and natural living. The Wooden Age, where bed and wall and door and house are made of pine-logs, where night is always cold, morning loud with rivers and cow-bells and existence balsam-sharp.

Today my deepest wish is to go to sleep for six months, if not for ever; it is an admission that life has become almost unendurable and that I must look to pleasure as a waking substitute for sleep. We cannot sleep twenty-four hours a day but we can at least make sleep and pleasure alternate, if once we will admit that, like deep narcotic treatment for nervous breakdown, they are remedies for the very sick. Reality, union with reality, is the true state of the soul when confident and healthy. Thus when Pope wrote:

> 'So slow the unprofitable Moments roll
> That lock up all the Functions of my soul;
> That keep me from Myself;'

he stated a profound truth. Unreality is what keeps us from ourselves and most pleasure is unreal.

In that dream of approaching forty I felt that I was about to die and became aware that I was no longer myself, but a creature inhabited entirely by parasites, a caterpillar infested by grubs of the ichneumon fly. Gin, whisky, sloth, fear, guilt, tobacco, had been appointed my inquilines; alcohol sloshed about within, while tendrils of melon and vine spread out from ear and nostril. My mind was a worn gramophone record, my true self was such a shadow as to seem non-existent and all this had taken place in the last three years.

Approaching forty. A glimpse of wisdom. 'Live in the present, Palinurus; you are too unbalanced to brood upon the past. One day you will remember nothing but its essence; now you must expel it from your mind.'

'The twelvemonth and a day being up,
    The dead began to speak:
"Oh who sits weeping on my grave,
    And will not let me sleep?"—

'"'Tis I, my love, sits on your grave,
    And will not let you sleep;
For I crave one kiss of your clay-cold lips,
    And that is all I seek."—

'"You crave one kiss of my clay-cold lips;
    But my breath smells earthy strong;
If you have one kiss of my clay-cold lips,
    Your time will not be long.

'"'Tis down in yonder garden green,
    Love, where we used to walk,
The finest flower that ere was seen
    Is wither'd to a stalk.

THE UNQUIET GRAVE

'"The stalk is wither'd dry, my love
So will our hearts decay;
So make yourself content, my love,
Till God calls you away."'[1]

Paris afternoons: The book-stall on the quai with old
prints that nobody wants, naughty novels corseted
in cellophane; the animal shop on the Quai de Gesvres;
ferrets, squirming and clucking in the straw, with red
eyes and little yawns which reveal their fine white teeth;
marmosets chattering over their stump of rotten banana,
moulting parrots; the mysterious ailing nocturnal
creature that I was always tempted to buy—'c'est un
binturong, monsieur'—and then the walk back over
the bridge; poplar leaves eddying in the yellow river;
misty black-and-grey streets of the Left Bank; discreet
shops full of *bibelots*, bad modern paintings, Empire
clocks.

Disorder of the hotel bedroom; books, drawings,
clothes and red plush; shadows lengthening, the desir-
able afternoon sleep with its bewildering nightmare-
starts and awakenings, its flash-backs to the past. Then
the purple neon sign shining in at the window and the
concierge on the telephone: 'Il y a quelqu'un en bas
qui vous demande'. 'Voulez-vous lui dire de monter.'

In youth the animal world obsessed me; I saw life
through creatures which were in a state of grace, creatures without remorse, without duties, without a past
or a future owning nothing but the intense present
and their eternal rhythm of hunger, sleep and play.
The ring-tailed lemurs with their reverence for the sun,
their leaps through the air and their howls of loneliness,
were dark Immortals of a primitive race; the ferrets
with their passionate blood-thirst and their tunnelling

[1] *Oxford Book of Ballads:* 'The Unquiet Grave'.

mania; the beautiful mute genette, the pine-marten, the racoons, the pitiful coati, the dying ocelot, the slow loris,—even the animals which I never owned, the beaver, otter, palm-civet and linsang,—these bright-fanged, saffron-throated aristocrats held the secret of life for me; they were clues to an existence without thought, guilt or ugliness wherein all was grace, appetite and immediate sensation: Impressionist materpieces which Nature flung upon the canvas of a day.

Now I care only for the Vegetable world; my day-dreams are no longer of otter-pool and sunny lemurarium, but of slobbering melon, downy quince and dew-dusted nectarine. I feel fruit trees to be an even stranger form of life and therefore more rewarding. Nothing is so alien, so unexpected in a tree as its fruit and yet by the fruit it is known; leaves, height and blossom are sacrificed; so by thinking, reading and maintaining an inner calm we too mature and ripen until the life which once flowered in such careless profusion is concentrated into husks, husks that, like pomegranates or the tomato on our window-sill, continue to mellow long after the leaf has fallen and the plant that bore them rotted to the ground.

'Good is the passive that obeys reason. Evil is the active springing from energy.'—BLAKE. It is more important, in fact, to be good than to do good because being, rather than doing, is the state which keeps us in tune with the order of things. Hence Pascal's reflection that all the evil of the world comes from men not being able to sit quietly in a room. Good is the retention of energy; evil a waste of it, energy which is taken away from growth. Like water, we are truest to our nature in repose.

'Tao is in the emptiness. Emptiness is the fast of the mind.'—CHUANG-TZU.

THE UNQUIET GRAVE

MASTERPLAY

Three thoughts from Eliot:

'Someone said: "The dead writers are remote from us because we *know* so much more than they did." Precisely, and they are that which we know.'

'What is to be insisted upon is that the poet must develop or procure the consciousness of the past and that he should continue to develop this consciousness throughout his career. What happens is a continual surrender of himself as he is at the moment to something which is more valuable. The progress of an artist is a continual self-sacrifice, a continual extinction of personality.'

'The more perfect the artist, the more completely separate in him will be the man who suffers and the mind which creates.'

The supreme liberty is liberty from the body, the last freedom is freedom from time; the true work of art the one which the seventh wave of genius throws far up the beach where the under-tow of time cannot drag it back. When all the motives that lead artists to create have fallen away, and the satisfactions of vanity and the play-instinct been exhausted, there remains the desire to construct that which has its own order, as a protest against the chaos to which all else appears condemned. While thought exists, words are alive and literature becomes an escape, not from, but into living.

Works of art which survive must all be indebted to the spirit of their age. Thus though Virgil and Horace copied Greek models, they imitated them at a time when the flowering of Roman civilization demanded just such a refinement, a taking over of the trusteeship of the past by the swelling Latin genius. In that sense every writer refashions the literature of the past and produces his tiny commentary, nothing is ever quite new; but there comes a moment when a whole culture ripens and prepares to make its own version of the great art of its predecessors.

The masterpieces appropriate to our time are in the style of the early Chirico, the later Rouault and Picasso's Guernica; sombre, magnificent yet personal statements of our tragedy; work of strong and noble architecture austerely coloured by loneliness and despair. Flaubert spoke true: to succeed a great artist must have both character and fanaticism and few in this country are willing to pay the price. Our writers have either no personality and therefore no style or a false personality and therefore a bad style; they mistake prejudice for energy and accept the sensation of material well-being as a system of thought.

The English language is like a broad river on whose bank a few patient anglers are sitting, while, higher up, the stream is being polluted by a string of refuse-barges tipping out their muck. The English language has, in fact, so contracted to our own littleness that it is no longer possible to make a good book out of words alone. A writer must concentrate on his vocabulary but must also depend on the order, the timing and spacing of his words, and try to arrange them in a form which is seemingly artless, yet perfectly proportioned. He must let a hiatus suggest that which the language will no longer accomplish. Words today are like the shells and rope of seaweed which a child brings home glistening from the beach and which in an hour have lost their lustre.

93

It is right proportion combined with simplicity of expression and seriousness of thought that enables a book to stand the test of time. To construct from the mind and to colour with the imagination a work which the judgement of unborn arbiters will consider perfect is the one immortality of which we can be sure. When we read the books of a favourite writer together with all that has been written about him, then his personality will take shape and leave his work to materialize through our own. The page will liberate its author; he will rise from the dead and become our friend. So is it with Horace, Montaigne, Sainte-Beuve, with Flaubert and Henry James: they survive in us, as we increase through them.

But these intimacies can be dangerous. For there are writers who lay seige to our personality, then storm the feeble garrison and occupy the citadel. Thus Flaubert, who appears at first our ally becomes, as we venture further into his work, the terrible Christos Pantocrator of our age with Sainte-Beuve his John the Baptist and George Sand his Magdalene. We relive his Passion with him, his Temptation, his Agony at Croisset, his Betrayal and Crucifixion by the Bourgeois; his letters become the Sermon on the Mount—'Tout est là; l'amour de l'Art'—and so we falter and faint and deny him thrice, in the Press, in the Ministry or on the Air,—until he rises before us in cold Norman wrath to pronounce 'Justice not mercy!' 'Un homme qui s'est institué artiste n'a plus le droit de vivre comme les autres.'

Flaubert on the Masterpiece
'Je me demande si un livre, indépendamment de ce qu'il dit, ne peut pas produire le même effet? (as the base of the Parthenon). Dans la précision des assemblages, la rareté des éléments, le poli de la surface,

94

l'harmonie de l'ensemble, n'y a-t-il pas une vertu intrinsèque, une espèce de force divine, quelque chose d'éternel comme un principe? (Je parle en platonicien.) Ainsi pourquoi y a-t-il un rapport nécessaire entre le mot juste et le mot musical? Pourquoi arrive-t-on toujours à faire un vers quand on resserre trop sa pensée? La loi des nombres gouverne donc les sentiments et les images, et ce qui paraît être l'extérieur est tout bonnement le dedans?'

September 10th: Full autumn magnificence; the green and gold streamers of the plane-tree waving transparently against the high sunlit sky. Birthday resolution: From now on specialize; never again make any concession to the ninety-nine parts of you which are like everybody else at the expense of the one which is unique. Never listen to the False Self talking.

'Le néant d'avoir quarante ans.'

September 15th: Entrée des coings.

> Pomifer autumnus fruges effuderit, et mox
> Bruma recurrit iners.[1]

ENEMIES OF ANGST

Flight to the country: the morning awakening of a house, noise of women in a courtyard, the chickens, ducks, geese and dogs being let out; the parrot stropping its beak on the bars of the cage; the smell of breakfast, the gardener bringing in tomatoes and lettuces; Sunday papers, taps running; and the drone of fighter-squadrons overhead. Lunch out of doors.

[1] Horace Odes, Book IV: 'Autumn, bringer of fruit, has poured out her riches, and soon sluggish winter returns.'

The afternoon nap, so rich in disturbances of memory; the bath in the fading daylight with hot-water pipes rumbling and shrieks of children going to bed, while the cold elmy sunshine westers over liquid fields. The sharp bed-time sortie into the night air.

It is only in the country that we can get to know a fellow-being or a book.

The mill where I sometimes stay provides another cure for Angst; the red lane through the Spanish chestnut wood, the apple trees on the lawn, the bees in the roof, the geese on the pond, the black sun-lit marsh marigolds, the wood-fire crackling in the low bedroom, the creak of the cellar-door and the recurrent monotonies of the silver-whispering weir,—what could be more womb-like or reassuring? Yet always the anxious owner is flying from it as from the scene of a crime.

Romantic surrealism and classical humanism, however antagonistic, are akin; they breed each other and the artist must contrive a synthesis. Blake and Pope or Flaubert and his mad 'Garçon' are complementary. The classical humanist is the parent, the surrealist the rebellious adolescent. Both are mother-fixed; only 'Social Realism' lies outside the family.

Surrealist and humanist differ as to what proportion of 'strangeness' (*le merveilleux*) is necessary as an ingredient of beauty and what proportion of violence is best suited to creative emotion.

Surrealism, the last international movement in the arts, is now in its decadence. Why? Because it borrowed the Communist idea of a small iron-disciplined élite without the appeal to the masses by which such discipline tries to justify itself. An æsthetic movement with a revolutionary dynamism and no popular appeal should proceed quite otherwise than by public scandal, publicity stunt, noisy expulsion and excommunication.

LA CLE DES CHANTS

For twenty years political mass-movements have absorbed the mounting sap of humanity. Surrealism, like its rival, classical humanism, is too romantic and too anti-industrial for the times. Our world has no use for liberal father or rebellious anarchist son. *Le merveilleux*, with the Sublime of the Humanists, belongs to the nineteenth-century past.

This is a pity, for as time goes on we see how Surrealism was revolutionary not only in the sense that all could take it home and practise there but as the last convulsion necessary to complete the French artistic-cycle, to tie the strands of classicism and romanticism, reason and imagination into a final knot, and so restore the clear head to the rebel heart.

Classical and romantic: private language of a family quarrel, a dead dispute over the distribution of emphasis between man and nature.

Abstract art denies both man and nature and thrives on the machine age; Naturalism refuses man all place while in Social Realism he dominates the picture.

Beware nevertheless of false dualities: classical and romantic, real and ideal, reason and instinct, mind and matter, male and female,—all should be merged into each other (as the Taoists merged their Yin and Yang into the Tao) and should be regarded as two aspects of one idea. Dualities which are defined at the same moment (stoic and epicurean, Whig and Tory) become united by the historical process, and end by having more, not less, in common. In a hundred years Science and Ethics (power and love), the present day duality, may seem as dead as the iota controversy, together with good and evil, free will and determinism, even space and time. Ideas which have for long divided individuals will become meaningless in the light of the forces that will separate groups.

THE UNQUIET GRAVE

Yet ridiculous as may seem the dualities in conflict at a given time, it does not follow that dualism is a worthless process. The river of truth is always splitting up into arms that reunite. Islanded between them the inhabitants argue for a lifetime as to which is the main-stream.

EARTH-LOVES OF THE EARTH BOUND: ENNOIA

Three or four people whom I have loved seem utterly set apart from all the rest; angelic, ageless creatures more alive than the living, embalmed perpetually in their all-devouring myth.

Ile de Gavrinis: Montagne de la Margeride: Auberge de Peyrebeilhe. 'Mar of murmury mermers in the mind . . .'

Clumps of rushes, brackish water, marram-grass, sea-thistles, *flore des dunes*,—Ile de Gavrinis over the green and violet ocean of the Morbihan. The dinghy grounds on white sand printed with the tails of lizards, the ancient lime avenue leads up to the lonely farm where a path winds among gorse and asphodel to the Presence of the Dead. There, in his Tumulus, lies the last Celtic prince, wrapped in his race's age-long death-wish; his great vault-stone carved with indecipherable warnings; runes of serpents and oak-leaves, of wave-eddies and wind-patterns, finger-prints of giant hands,—O power-less to save! And that night in Vannes, the cave-wedding —*Summoque ulularunt vertice Nymphæ.*[1] She with sad grave gem-like beauty and happiness soon to be thrown away.

Leaving Bellac after crossing for two days the plains of the sandy Loire, we enter the Bocage Limousin,

[1] The nymphs wailed from the top of the hill. (An air-raid warning.)

traverse a country of tall tree-hedges blueing into the pale spring sky and reach the first hills, the Blond mountains, forest beginnings of the Châtaigneraie. A new strip of maps and the sun always warmer; mountain nights in stone buildings, melted snow in the running water, darker wine in the inns, deeper beds. Rivers tumbling through towns; rain-drenched chestnuts green in the swinging lights of Tulle; Mauriac, Sainte-Flour, Saint-Chély-d'Apcher; snow-driven moorlands of the Margeride, pine-forests of Velay and Vivarais; cloud-shadows over the Gerbier de Jonc. There on the edge of the tableland stands the haunted Auberge de Peyrebeilhe, (where once so few came out who went in.)[1] But now the low room with blackened ceiling has grown less dangerous to lovers than the almond-blossom airs of the warm Ardéche, than the limestone chasm leading down to civilization where the Furies are awaiting Ennoia and happiness is thrown away.

'Courage is not simply *one* of the virtues but the form of every virtue at the testing point, which means at the point of highest reality.'—C. S. LEWIS.

Cowardice in living: without health and courage we cannot face the present or the germ of the future in the present and take refuge in evasion. Evasion through comfort, society, through acquisitiveness, through the book-bed-bath defence system, above all through the flight to the romantic womb of history, into primitive myth-making. The refusal to include the great mass-movements of the twentieth century in our art or our myth will drive us to take refuge in the past; in surrealism, magic, primitive religion or eighteenth-century wonderlands. We fly to Mediterranean womb-pockets and

[1] The innkeeper and his coloured wife used to murder their guests.

dream-islands, into dead controversy and ancient hermetic bric-à-brac, like a child who sits hugging his toys and who screams with rage when told to put on his boots.

Realities of our time.

> History constructed out of global blocks.
> The Decline of Europe.
> Anglo-American rivalry and imperialism.
> Russian Managerial imperialism.
> Chinese or Japanese imperialism.
> English National Suburbanism.
> The Great American Vacuum.
> Massacres and atrocities, poverty, famine.

'Well, which side are you on? The Corn-Goddess or the Tractor? The Womb or the Bulldozer? Christ, Freud, Buddha, Baudelaire, Bakunin, or Marx, Watson, Pavlov, Stalin, Shaw? Come clean, moody Palinurus, no synthesis this time and no Magic Circle either? We need men like you in the Group Age. Will you take your turn at the helm as you used to? Remember?

> Princeps gubernator densum Palinurus agebat
> Agmen?[1]

or do you prefer to daydream in the lavatory, *petit coin sombre* of the Bourgeois Formalist, while a new world is being born?

How do you react to our slogan 'Total Everybody Always'? Have you at last understood that your miserable failure as an individual is proof that you pursue a lost cause? Man invents God when he loses his Party

[1] 'Ahead of all the Master Pilot steer'd.'

Card. He is neither angel, nor beast, nor as you with your mystique of sloth would make him even a vegetable, but a social unit, a cell, and as such will find fulfilment only through participation in the communal life of an organized group.'

Answer: 'In my beginning is my end.' As the acorn contains the oak or the folded kernel of the Spanish chestnut implies the great whorled bole and serrated leaf of the full-grown tree, so each human being possesses a form appropriate to him which time will educate and ripen. 'Tout est dans la semence': the acorns will not make a hedge nor the chestnuts an avenue; we are born with certain shapes ahead of us, certain ideas to fulfil; to seek unity or bring out diversity; to attack tradition or perpetuate lost causes; to build the future or to exhume our spiritual ancestors, and derive hope and inspiration from them; to discover certain places, to love and lose certain faces or to develop an immediate antipathy to others. If I had been a true product of the age your question could never have arisen. My rôle is not of the future but, like Eliot's poet, "to live in what is not merely the present, but the present moment of the past." I believe that a conscious affinity with Nature forms the shield of Perseus through which man can affront the Gorgon of his fate and that, in the territaries of the future where humanity cements itself up from the light of the sun, this dragon-slaying mirror will rust and tarnish. So I have nothing to say to the masses or to the machines, to bosses or bureaucrats, States or statistics, Nations or Parties. I am but a link in the chain of individual heretics and failures, a wood-wind solo in the interminable symphony, drowned at once by the brass and percussion but necessary to the composer's score. An interpreter between intellect and imagination, between reason and the physical world,

THE UNQUIET GRAVE

I tend the graves,—*sapientum templa serena*—of Horace and Tibullus, of Pythagoras and Aristippus, of Montaigne and Lao-Tsu; I speak the language of animals and enjoy the confidence of the vegetable powers.

And I answer a seven-fold 'No' to your question: A physiological no, because I am not a cell, but myself. A biological no, because a specialized mutation from the norm indicates the richness and vitality of the species. A sociological no, because those who lack the herd-instinct are generally in advance of the herd which is conservative, stupid, intolerant and bourgeois. A psychological no, because those who have been all their lives used to intellectual isolation are the ones best fitted to remain isolated; they grow adjusted to their mal-adjustment. A political no, for England will remain the smallest of the great powers and so must depend for her survival on qualitative standards. An æsthetic no, because the practice of literature is still best carried through the individual unit. An ethical no, because I do not 'find fulfilment through participation in the communal life of an organized group',—that is tyranny,—but in the pursuit of art and knowledge and by communion with the Bourgeois Formalism of Nature. To sum up: I agree with Flaubert, 'A mesure que l'humanité se perfectionne, l'homme se dégrade.'

October. Quince days. Io Lemuria![1]

Departure of my tormentors. Philosophic calm, soaring Hope, manic exaltation, mysterious freedom from Angst. Dare I suppose that a cure has been accom-

[1] Roman festival designed to propitiate the Lemures or wandering evil spirits of the dead. Once a year as on our All Souls Eve, they hungrily revisit their loved ones. Broad Beans (a most suggestive vegetable) were thrown to them as an appeasement offering after which they were requested to leave. 'Manes exite Paterni!' Ovid. Fasti, Bk. v.

plished, the bones of Palinurus buried and his ghost laid? For once it seems that the past has fallen away like the mantle of snow from a creaking fir-tree.

> 'As for the Dog, the Furies and their Snakes
> The gloomy Caverns or the burning Lakes
> And all the vain infernal trumpery
> They neither are, nor were, nor e'er can be.'

There is no hate without fear. Hate is crystallized fear, fear's dividend, fear objectivized. We hate what we fear and so where hate is, fear will be lurking. Thus we hate what threatens our person, our liberty, our privacy, our income, our popularity, our vanity and our dreams and plans for ourselves. If we can isolate this element in what we hate we may be able to cease from hating. Analyse in this way the hatred of ideas or of the kind of people whom we have once loved and whose faces are preserved in Spirits of Anger. Hate is the consequence of fear; we fear something before we hate; the child who fears noises becomes the man who hates them.

'Whatever you blame, that you have done yourself.'— GRODDECK.

Dark saying of La Rochefoucauld: 'Le seul honnête homme est celui qui ne se pique de rien'.

'Ce serait avoir gagné beaucoup dans la vie que de savoir rester toujours parfaitement naturel et sincère avec soi-même, de ne croire aimer que ce qu'on aime véritablement, et de ne pas prolonger par amour-propre et par émulation vaine des passions déjà expirées.' —SAINTE-BEUVE.

THE UNQUIET GRAVE

FAREWELL TO SAINTE-BEUVE

'Le souvenir est comme une plante qu'il faut avoir plantée de bonne heure ensemble; sans quoi elle ne s'enracine pas.'

'Les lieux les plus vantés de la terre sont tristes et désenchantés lorsqu'on n'y porte plus ses espérances.'

'Quelle que soit la diversité des points de départ les esprits des capables de mûrir arrivent, plus qu'on ne croit, aux mêmes résultats; combien de gens meurent avant d'avoir fait le tour d'eux-mêmes.'

'Je ne suis complètement moi que plume en main et dans le silence du cabinet.'

A child, left to play alone, says of quite an easy thing, 'Now I am going to do something very difficult'. Soon, out of vanity, fear and emptiness, he builds up a world of custom, convention and myth in which everything must be just so; certain doors are one-way streets, certain trees sacred, certain paths taboo. Then along comes a grown-up or a more robust child; they kick over the imaginary wall, climb the forbidden tree, regard the difficult as easy and the private world is destroyed. The instinct to create myth, to colonize reality with the emotions, remains. The myths become tyrannies until they are swept away, when we invent new tyrannies to hide our suddenly perceived nakedness. Like caddis-worms or like those crabs which dress themselves with seaweed, we wear belief and custom.

Taoists believe that devotion to anything except Nature ages them and therefore live simply on hill-sides or near forests, like the sage whose wants were so few that when he decided to leave his cottage he found the brambles round it had grown too high for him to pass. But what becomes of loving Nature if Nature does not want us? Let us go for a walk on the moors; at first the high pure air, the solitude under the hot sun where the burns splash and the grouse shrieks, purge us of our city poison until art and civilization seem oppressive and vulgar, rainbow hues on the dying mullet, occupations which cut man off from his primitive vegetation-cult. Then as the day gets hotter and we stumble on over scruffy heather and bubbling bog there is a change; Nature would seem not to share in our communion and to prefer her own backward progeny; the grouse's cackle, raven, falcon, mountain hare, the noisy burn, the whole hill-side in the hot afternoon become ominous and hostile—archaic emblems of Ennui—something we have long grown out of. Once more the craving revives for architecture, art and the intellect. By the evening it is raining and, after the visit to our great, gross, unappreciative Mother, we are glad to be back with our books and fire-side conversation. It is to Civilization, not to Nature that man must return.

The Vegetable Conspiracy: Man is now on his guard against insect parasites; against liver-flukes, termites, Colorado beetles, but has he given thought to the possibility that he has been selected as the target of vegetable attack, marked down by the vine, hop, juniper, the tobacco plant, tea-leaf and coffee-berry for destruction? What willing converts these Jesuits of the gastric juices make,—and how cleverly they retain them! Does a smoker consider the menace of the weed spreading in his garden, will a drunkard read the warning of the ivy round the oak? What populations fear the seed-strangling rubber or have recorded the increasing mortality caused by punctures from the rose? And what of gold, that slow mineral poison?

Money talks through the rich as alcohol swaggers in the drunken, calling softly to itself to unite into the lava flow which petrifies all it touches.

No one would start to play a game without knowing the rules. Yet most of us play the interminable game of life without any because we have no idea what they are. But there are only two possible systems according to whether or not we believe in God. If we believe that the universe is an accident and life an accident contingent on the universe and man an accident contingent on life; then rules are made for men to be happy and it has been found by generations of exponents that happiness consists in fulfilment of the personality—in former days through the family, now by rendering more and more services to a group—in fact through the happiness of the greatest number. This is the game as played by Epicurus, Holbach, Marx, Mill, Bentham, Comte, and William James.

If, however, we believe in God, then our duty is to do His will and not our own and our conception of the rules varies with our conception of His nature. But whatever this conception is we are united in the belief that the success or failure of our life as such cannot be estimated by any utilitarian standard.

Faced, then, with these completely different systems for this all-important game, can we not find out once and for all whether there is a God; whether He had strewn clues over the universe for man to pick up or whether we ourselves have invented Him, as a useful three-letter expression for anything which remains outside our knowledge?

The answer seems to rest with three categories of thinkers; the physicists, who incline to believe in God but are now all busy making explosives; the biologists and chemists who can produce almost everything except life and who, if they could create life, would prove that it might once have arisen accidentally; and the psychologists and physiologists, who are struggling to discover the relation of mind to brain, the nature of consciousness.

A baby, after an exhibition on the pot, with much anger and howling, stretches out her arms with a little cry, as when her pram is passing under trees, to reveal an immense wonder and love for life,—a Soul. I have read that the cuckoo enters the world with two advantages over other birds; a special muscle on its back for throwing them from the nest; and a cry which is irresistible to the foster-parents. This sudden cry of recognition and pleasure is what keeps us all on the go from grab-all to crave. *Volupté*! The eternal cuckoo call.

'O fins d'automne, hivers, printemps trempés de boue,
Endormeuses saisons ' . . .

Tout mon mal vient de Paris. There befell the original sin and the original ecstasy; there were the holy places— the Cross-Roads and the Island. Quai Bourbon, Rue de Vaugirard, Quai d'Anjou.

Air: *Transfrétons la Sequane*!

'Nous transfrétons le Sequane au dilicule et crepuscule; nous déambulons par les compites et quadriviers de l'urbe, nous déspumons la verbocination latiale.'

Evening in June: walking down the Rue Vavin, past the shop with ivory canes in the window, away from the polyglot bedlam of Montparnasse into the Luxembourg garden where children are playing croquet under the black-trunked chestnuts and wool-green catalpas, then out at the corner where the Rue Servandoni's leaning mansards join the sombre Rue de Vaugirard. On by the book-booths of the Odéon, by the shimmering Fontaine de Medicis and the diners in the open air, then through the broad melancholy twilight of the Rue Soufflot to the cold splendour of the Panthéon, past the blistered shutters of the Hôtel des Grands Hommes. There, behind the church, the Rue de la Montagne Sainte-Geneviève, Via Sacra of the Latin Quarter, winds steeply down the Founder's holy hill.

In the doorways sit families on their wooden chairs, while from the Bal Musette where *Fiesta* began the Java fades on the sultry air; then across the Rue des Ecoles with its groaning trams, and so by the stews and noisy wine-shops of the Place Maubert to meet the Seine at the Quai de la Tournelle.

Quai Bourbon. Miserere. The Ile Saint-Louis strains at her moorings, the river eddies round the stone prow where tall poplars stand like masts, and mist rises about the decaying houses which seventeenth-century nobles raised on their meadows. Yielding asphalt, sliding waters; long windows with iron bars set in damp walls; anguish and fear. Rendez-vous des Mariniers, Hôtel de Lauzun: moment of the night when the saint's blood liquefies, when the leaves shiver and presentiments of loss stir within the dark coil of our fatality.

'Porque sabes que siempre te he querido.'

Quai Bourbon, Quai d'Orléans, Quai d'Anjou.

Then came the days of ferrets with ribs like wish-bones for whom we bought raw liver from the horse-butcher in the Rue de Seine while they tunnelled round the octagonal room in the Hôtel de la Louisiane. They pursued oranges, eggs and ping-pong balls and wore harness with little bells; and from their number came

forth a queen, the tawny, docile Norfolk beauty whom
we named the English Rose, who performed her cycle
of eating, playing, sleeping and relieving herself and
who saw three continents from a warm sleeve. She
hunted the Rue Monge and the Rue Mouffetard, the
courts of the Val de Grace and the gardens of the
Observatoire, the Passage des Princes and the Place
de Fürstenberg. She searched the Parc Montsouris
and the Buttes-Chaumont, the doss-houses of the Rue
Quincampoix and the Boulevard de la Chapelle; she
visited the tattered buildings in the Rue de la Goutte
d'Or and heard the prostitutes calling to each other
from their beds in the Rue de la Charbonnière; she
explored the gilt, the plush, the columns and flaking
ceilings of the Deuxième Arrondissement, the arcades
of the Palais-Royal and the Place des Victoires, the
corner-houses, razor-sharp, in the Rue de la Lune.
She sniffed at all the gates of Paris: Porte Saint-Denis,
Porte d'Orléans, Porte des Lilas; pocket gardens of
the Gobelin workers along the Bièvre, exposed tendons
of the Nord railway by the Boulevard Barbès and ware-
houses on the Saint-Martin Canal. Yet most she loved,
a short walk from her couch of straw, the stony public
garden by Saint-Germain-des-Prés.

And many bars where sad-eyed barmen told the seasons
by clipping chits for 'grogs-américains' and 'champagne-
oranges', and many restaurants, now closed and forgotten, understood her favourite diet of raw egg. The
Moine Gourmet, the Restaurant de la Chaise with its
Burgundy and Lesbians, Montagné's perfection, Foyot's
dying autumnal grandeur, Madame Genot's austere
bistro with her home-grown wines, Rosalie's fresh corn,
Lafon's pâté, Marius' pellucid Beaujolais,—in all of
these she clucked approval.

And many *boîtes* once made her welcome: the Bateau

Ivre in the Place de l'Odéon, the old Bœuf, Melody's and the Grand Ecart, the trellised galleries of the Bal Blomet and the Stygian reaches of the Magic River in Luna-Park. Love came to her in Hampshire and she was covered, and in Toulon gave birth to nine fine youngsters in the hotel bath. She would wash them and clean up their droppings till ambivalence was engendered when, to escape their demands, she would climb on to my lap, looking up at us with pale golden eyes and yawning to show that nothing was changed. Then one day, being hungry, she strayed from the garden and entered a cottage kitchen, where she sat up to beg as we had taught her—until the ignorant peasants kicked her to death and brought back her limp body; filthy-hearted women;—'Oui, monsieur, on a bien vu qu'elle n'a pas voulu mourir.'

It was after the reign of the English Rose that our days were darkened by the graves of the lemurs; on distant shores they lie,—far from Madagascar, yet never far from the rocks where the flowering cistus out-blanches the salt-encrusting spray.

'Living for beauty',—October on the Mediterranean; blue sky scoured by the mistral, red and golden vine branches, wind-fretted waves chopping round the empty yachts; plane-trees peeling; palms rearing up their dingy underlinen; mud in the streets and from doorways at night the smell of burning oil. Through the dark evening I used to bicycle in to fetch our dinner, past the harbour with its bobbing launches and the cafés with their signs banging. At the local restaurant there would be one or two 'plats à emporter', to which I would add some wine, sausage and Gruyère cheese, a couple of 'Diplomates' to smoke and a new 'Détective' or 'Chasseur Français'; then I would bowl back heavy-laden with the mistral behind me, a lemur buttoned up inside my jacket with his head sticking out. Up the steep drive it was easy to be blown off into the rosemary, then dinner would be spoilt. We ate it with our fingers beside the fire,—true beauty lovers,—then plunged into the advertisements in *Country Life*, dreaming of that Priory at Wareham where we would end our days. 'Living for Beauty' entailed a busy life of answering advertisements, writing for prospectuses, for information about cottages in Hampstead, small manors in the West—or else for portable canoes, converted Dutch barges 'that could go through the Canals', second-hand yachts, caravans and cars. Homesick, we liked best the detective stories, because they reeked of whisky, beefsteaks, expresses from Paddington, winter landscapes, old inns and Georgian houses that screen large gardens off the main street of country towns. There live the solicitors and doctors and clever spinsters who brew home-made poison and who come into their own in these exacting tales, there arrive for summer the artist from London and the much-consulted military man. At last we would go to bed, bolting the doors while the lemurs cried in the moonlight, house-ghosts bounding from the mulberries to the palms, from the palms to the tall pines whose cones the dormice nibble, from the pines to the roof, and so to our bedroom window where they would press their eager faces to the pane. In the bathroom one of us would be washing while the other crammed fir-cones in the stove. The stove roars, the water is heated and the room fills with steamy fragrance. The two lemurs are admitted and worm their way down to sleep in the bottom of the bed. In the early morning, while we dream of Wareham, they will creep out round our feet, seize the aromatic tooth-paste in their long black gloves, jump through the window and spring with it down to the sunny earth.

THE UNQUIET GRAVE

When I think of lemurs depression engulfs me 'à peu que le cœur ne me fend'. As W. H. Hudson says, 'they have angel's eyes' and they die of 'flu.

GRAVES OF THE LEMURS

Whoopee. Gentle and fearless, he passed four leafy years in the South of France. He would chase large dogs, advancing backwards and glaring through his hind legs, then jump chittering at them and pull their tails. He died through eating a poisoned fig laid down for rats. The children who saw him take the fruit tried to coax it from him, but he ran up a tree with it. There they watched him eat and die.

Polyp. Most gifted of lemurs, who hated aeroplanes in the sky, on the screen and even on the wireless. How he would have hated this war! He could play in the snow or swim in a river or conduct himself in a night-club; he judged human beings by their voices; biting some, purring over others, while for one or two well-seasoned old ladies he would brandish a black prickle-studded penis, shaped like an eucalyptus seed. Using his tail as an aerial, he would lollop through long grass to welcome his owners, embracing them with little cries and offering them a lustration from his purple tongue and currycomb teeth. His manners were those of some spoiled young Maharajah, his intelligence not inferior, his heart all delicacy,—women, gin and muscats were his only weaknesses. Alas, he died of pneumonia while we scolded him for coughing, and with him vanished the sea-purple cicada kingdom of calanque and stone-pine and the concept of life as an arrogant private dream shared by two.

.   .   .   .   .

As the French soldier said of the Chleuhs in Morocco, 'Je les aime et je les tue'. So it is with the lemurs, black and grey bundles of vitality, eocene ancestors from whom we are all descended, whose sun-greeting call some hold to be the origin of the word 'Ra' and thus of human language,—we have treated these kings in exile as we used Maoris and Marquesas islanders or the whistling Guanches of Teneriffe,—all those golden island-races, famous for beauty, whom Europe has taken to its shabby heart to exploit and ruin.

To have set foot in Lemuria is to have been close to the mysterious sources of existence, to have known what it is to live wholly in the present, to soar through the green world four yards above the ground, to experience sun, warmth, love and pleasure as intolerably as we glimpse them in a waking dream, and to have heard that heart-rendering cry of the lonely or abandoned which goes back to our primaeval dawn. Wild ghost faces from a lost continent who soon will be extinct. . . .

And 'living for beauty': in one lovely place always pining for another; with the perfect woman imagining one more perfect; with a bad book unfinished beginning a second, while the almond tree is in blossom, the grass-hopper fat and the winter night disquieted by the plock and gurgle of the sea,—that too would seem extinct for ever.

'Your time is short, watery Palinurus. What do you believe?'

'I believe in two-faced truth, in the Either, the Or and the Holy Both. I believe that if a statement is true then its opposite must be true. (Aristotle: 'The knowledge of opposites is one.') Thus now (November the eleventh) I am again interested in philosophy, psychology, and religion and am reading about Gnosticism, most exquisite and insidious of heresies and once more find myself among its charms and amulets; its snake-god ABRASAX, and the Gnostic theory that Adam in the Garden of Eden was the babe in the womb fed by four rivers (arteries from the navel), and expelled from his mother into the world at the Fall. This time a year ago I was interested in these same ideas, reading Lao-Tsu with as much passion as I now read Epicurus (and now I find that Lao-Tsu was called 'The Chinese Epicurus'), so that it is more true to say that this is the time of year when religions are interested in me. Or is it that in late autumn the season forbids an active existence, and so we are forced back on reading and contemplation, on those schemes of thought which imply a corresponding rejection of the world?

To attain two-faced truth we must be able to resolve all our dualities, simultaneously to perceive life as comedy and tragedy, to see the mental side of the physical and the reverse. We must learn to be at the same time objective and subjective—like Flaubert, who enjoyed what Thibaudet called 'la pleine logique artistique de la vision binoculaire', or with that 'double focus' which Auden beautifully describes in *New Year Letter*.

Today the function of the artist is to bring imagination to science and science to imagination, where they meet, in the myth.[1]

---

[1] Gide gives the perfect two-faced myth-truth about religion (*Attendu que . . .* Algiers 1943):
'Il ne peut être question de deux Dieux. Mais je me garde, sous ce nom de Dieu, de confondre deux choses trés différentes; différentes jusqu'à s'opposer: D'une part l'ensemble du Cosmos et des lois naturelles qui le régissent; matière et forces, énergies; cela c'est le côté Zeus; et l'on peut bien appeler cela Dieu, mais c'est en enlevant à ce mot toute signification personnelle et morale. D'autre part le faisceau de tous le efforts humains vers le bien, vers le beau, la lente maîtrisation de ces forces brutales et leur mise en service pour réaliser le bien et le beau sur la terre; ceci, c'est le côté Prométhée; et c'est le côté

Now that I seem to have attained a temporary calm, I understand how valuable unhappiness can be; melancholy and remorse form the deep leaden keel which enables us to sail into the wind of reality; we run aground sooner than the flat-bottomed pleasure-lovers but we venture out in weather that would sink them and we choose our direction. What distinguishes true civilization from the mass-fabricated substitutes except that tap-root to the Unconscious, the sense of original sin? What artist-philosopher except Voltaire and Goethe has been without it?

'Voilà ce que tous les socialistes du monde n'ont pas voulu voir avec leur éternelle prédication matérialiste, ils ont nié la *douleur*, ils ont blasphémé les trois quarts de la poésie moderne; le sang du Christ qui se remue en nous, rien ne l'extirpera, rien ne le tarira, il ne s'agit pas de le dessécher, mais de lui faire des ruisseaux. Si le sentiment de l'insuffisance humaine, du néant de la vie, venait à périr (ce qui serait la conséquence de leur hypothèse) nous serions plus bêtes que les oiseaux qui au moins perchent sur les arbres.'—FLAUBERT.

If we apply depth-psychology to our own lives we see how enslaved we remain to the womb and the mother. Womb of Mother Church, of Europe, mother of continents, of horseshoe harbour and valley, of the lap of earth, of the bed, the arm-chair and the bath or of the Court of Charles II, of Augustan London, or the Rome of Cicero; of the bow-window of the club, of the house by the lake or water-front sacred to Venus;—

Christ aussi bien; c'est l'épanouissement de l'homme et toutes les vertus y concourent. Mais ce Dieu n'habite nullement la nature; il n'existe que dans l'homme et par l'homme; il est créé par l'homme, ou si vous préférez, c'est à travers l'homme qu'il se crée; et tout effort reste vain, pour l'extérioriser par la prière.'

all our lives seeking a womb with a view. Knowing this weakness we can make allowance for it in our thinking, aware that these reassuring apron-symbols have their parallel in certain sets of ideas; particularly in the half-mystical and theological, half-legendary beliefs and prejudices which we derive from the classical world and which form a kind of old wives' tale or maternal substitute for the vigour and audacity of constructive thought. Thus I fulfil the childhood pattern of making little expeditions into the world outside my myth-mother and then running back to her warmth. Yet in these days it is important for an artist to grasp that the logical exploratory voyage of reason is the finest process of the mind. Every other activity is a form of regression,—'Penser fait la grandeur de l'homme'. Thus the much vaunted 'night-mind', the subconscious world of myth and nostalgia, of child-imagination and instinctual drives, though richer, stranger and more absorbing than the world of reason, as Isis than Apollo, nevertheless owes its strength to our falling back on all that is primitive and infantile; it is an act of cowardice to the God in Man.

Man exudes a sense of reverence like a secretion. He smears it over everything and so renders a place like Stonehenge or the lake of Nemi (Diana's mirror) particularly sacred,—yet the one can become a petrol-station and the other be drained by a megalomaniac; no grove is too holy to be cut down. When we are tired or ill, our capacity for reverence, like our capacity for seeing the difficulty of things, increases till it becomes a kind of compulsion-neurosis or superstition; therefore it would seem that the mythoclasts are always right,—until we know what these mother-haters, these savagers of the breast, will worship in their turn. Lenin, the father figure mummified, replaces the Byzantine Christ. Reverence and destruction alternate; therefore the wise two-faced

116

man will reverence destructively, like Alaric or Akbar, and like Gibbon, Renan, Gide, reverently destroy.

Example of destructive reverence: *Un Chien Andalou*.[1]

Studio Vingt-Huit—high up a winding street of Montmartre in the full blasphemy of a freezing Sunday; taxis arriving, friends greeting each other, an excitable afternoon audience. In the hall stands a surrealist book-stall, behind is a bar where a gramophone plays 'Ombres Blanches' and disturbing sardanas while beyond is a small modern theatre. The lights are lowered and the film begins: 'Prologue'; 'Once upon a time' [I quote from the script], 'a balcony was in the dark. Indoors a man was whetting his razor. He looked up through the window at the sky and saw a fleecy cloud drawing near to the full moon. Then a young girl's head with staring eyes. Now the fleecy cloud passes over the moon. And the razor-blade passes through the girl's eye, slicing it in two.—End of Prologue.' The audience gasp—and there appear the beautiful haunted creatures,—Pierre Batchef as the young man, the cyclist, with his intellectual distinction and romantic depravity, then his Spanish-looking heroine. And the lovely girl in the street, who picks up the severed hand with the painted fingers! 'She must at that very moment register an extraordinary emotion which completely distracts her. She is as if entranced by echoes of some far-off church music, perhaps it is the music she has heard in earliest child-hood . . . She remains rooted to the spot in utter contri-tion. Motor-cars flash by at break-neck speed. Suddenly she is run over by one and horribly mutilated. There-upon, with the firmness of one doing what he is fully

[1] 'Un Chien Andalou was the film of adolescence and death which I was going to plunge right into the heart of Paris with all the weight of an Iberian dagger.'—DALI: *Autobiography*.

entitled to do, the cyclist comes up to the other and, having gazed lecherously straight into her eyes, puts his hand on her jumper over her breasts. Close-up of the eager hands touching the breasts. These themselves appear through the jumper. Thereupon the cyclist's face is seen to take on a look of terrible, almost mortal anguish, and blood dribbles from his mouth on to the girl's bared breast.'

So the film hurries to its end where the woman and her cyclist lover 'lie buried up to their necks in the limitless desert, blind and ragged, roasted by the sun and eaten by a swarm of insects'. This contemptuous private world of jealousy and lust, of passion and aridity, whose beautiful occupants patter about like stoats in search of blood, produced an indescribable effect, a tremendous feeling of excitement and liberation. The Id had spoken and,— through the obsolete medium of the silent film,—the spectators had been treated to their first glimpse of the fires of despair and frenzy which were smouldering beneath the complacent post-war world.

The picture was received with shouts and boos and when a pale young man tried to make a speech, hats and sticks were flung at the screen. In one corner a woman was chanting 'Salopes, salopes, salopes!' and soon the audience began to join in. With the impression of having witnessed some infinitely ancient horror, Saturn swallowing his sons, we made our way out into the cold of February 1929, that unique and dazzling cold.[1]

Why does this strong impression still persist? Because *Un Chien Andalou* brought out the grandeur of the conflict inherent in romantic love, the truth that the heart is made to be broken, and after it has mended, to be broken again. For romantic love, the supreme intoxica-

[1] 'A date in the history of the Cinema, a date marked in blood.'—*Montes* (Dali: *Autobiography*).

tion of which we are capable, is more than an intensifying of life; it is a defiance of it and belongs to those evasions of reality through excessive stimulus which Spinoza called 'titivations'. By the law of diminishing returns our desperate century forfeits the chance of being happy and, because it finds happiness insipid, our world is regressing to chaos.

Why? Because, as in the days of the Delphic Oracle, happiness consists in temperance and self-knowledge, and these are now beyond the reach of ordinary people who, owing to the pursuit of violent sensation, can no longer distinguish between pleasure and pain.

'Happiness is the only sanction of life; where happiness fails, existence remains a mad and lamentable experiment,' writes Santayana, which is but a restatement of Aristotle's definition that happiness, not goodness, is the end of life: 'we choose happiness for itself, and never with a view to anything further; whereas we choose honour, pleasure, intellect, because we believe that through them we shall be made happy.' Yet at once the ring of the words 'mad and lamentable' drowns the definition. A 'mad and lamentable experiment' seems to us more compulsive, more beguiling, and more profound in its appeal. Compare Aristotle and Santayana with a mental specialist, Doctor Devine. I quote from his *Recent Advances in Psychiatry*:

'Sometimes the development of a delusion leads to a cessation of tension, and is associated with a feeling of tranquillity and certainty, such as the patient had not hitherto experienced. A study of the past history of these cases sometimes creates the impression that the whole life had been converging to its solution in the psychosis in an inevitable kind of way. It is not unusual for a patient to say that his whole life had been like a dream and that now he feels awake for the first time. The delusion is, as it were, the inspiration for which he had long been waiting. . . . Something altogether unique is created in a psychosis; the mind is invaded by morbid mental growths.'

Thus in opposition to Aristotle's definition of happiness as an intensifying of the life of reason, we can oppose the existence of these illusion-ridden patients, the paraphrenics who have 'achieved a state of permanent bio-psychic equilibrium at the expense of their reason'— and there are also schizophrenes and manic-depressives whose lives are rich and crowded above the normal. To quote Dr. Devine: 'The schizophrenic does not suffer from a loss of something, he suffers from a surfeit, psychologically his consciousness is fuller than normal consciousness and the reality which it embraces is more thickly populated than that comprehended by the normal mind. . . . The conscious personality plays a passive role as far as the development of his psychosis is concerned and can do nothing to control what is happening within his organism.'

This moth-and-candle preoccupation with the Morbid Mind is but one of the Approaches to Pain which nowadays seem so rich in glamour. Insanity beckons us to fulfil high destinies and to recognize our paraphrenic vocation. Milder forms of manic-depression withdraw the over-sensitive from circulation to let them off lightly with an anxiety-neurosis or nervous breakdown; tuberculosis offers some a prolonged ecstasy; alcohol clowns others into oblivion; stomach-ulcers, piles and colitis provide us with honourable excuses; impotence or frigidity can always be relied upon to stop the cheque and every degree of fever is at hand to send up our emotional temperature. And what illness performs for the indivi-

dual, war accomplishes for the mass, until total war
succeeds in plunging the two thousand million inhabitants of the globe into a common nightmare.

Why? 'Because,' say the priests, 'men have forgotten
God'; 'wanting the Pilot and Palinure of reason and
religion they runne themselves upon the rocks';
'because,' say the materialists, 'they have neglected
economic principles'; 'because,' says a philosopher, 'a
madman at Sils Maria once wrote a book which, fifty
years later, inspired another in Munich'. Or because we
blindly enjoy destruction and can think of nothing
better, since for us

'Le printemps adorable a perdu son odeur'?

Why do we like war? Is it that all men would revenge
themselves for their betrayal by their mothers and of
their mothers, hitting out blindly to efface the memory
of the triple expulsion—expulsion from the sovereignty
of the womb, from the sanctuary of the breast, from the
intoxication of the bed and the lap?

No, it is not just through our weaning that we learn to use
our teeth on one another, nor even from the terrible rebuff
which we can still remember when our mother began to
reject our advances and we were packed off to the living
death of school, so much as by that more subtle conditioning which Freud analyses in *Beyond the Pleasure
Principle*. There he argues that certain patterns of childhood unhappiness and separation are re-enacted in later
life. 'Thus one knows people with whom every relationship ends in the same way: benefactors whose protégés
invariably after a time desert them in ill-will, men with
whom every friendship ends in the friend's treachery,
lovers whose tender relationships with women each and
all run through the same phases and come to the same

end . . . in the light of such observations as these, we may venture to make the assumption that there really exists in psychic-life a repetition-compulsion which goes beyond the pleasure principle'. In *Civilization and Its Discontents* Freud considers all prevailing nostrums for happiness and finds them wanting; in our culture Eros and the Death-wish fight it out; in our civilization there is a Superego which makes us all feel guilty and a repressive and anal element in the bureaucratic tidiness, caution, and frugality of the society which we have made.

Yet to blame society or the tyranny of the herd is but to distribute the blame on the individual in a more general way. If we had all enjoyed happy childhoods with happy parents, then prisons, barracks and asylums would be empty. The herd would be kinder, society wiser, the world would be changed. Man, however, is complete not only through being well adjusted to humanity; humanity must also be adjusted to the non-human, to the Nature which it perpetually thwarts and outrages, to the indifferent Universe. In Gide's use of the myth, Prometheus must come to terms with Zeus. If we return to our fortunate madmen, not to the remorse-stricken melancholiacs, but to those who are happier for their renunciation of the external world, we find that they are happy because 'they have achieved permanent bio-psychic equilibrium at the expense of their reason'.

In other words, bio-psychic equilibrium is such an intense and unfailing source of happiness that the loss of their reason and of all personal contact with reality are a small price for these Taoists to pay. Now this bio-psychic equilibrium is but that sensation of harmony with the universe, of accepting life and of being part of nature which we experience in childhood and which afterwards we discover through love, artistic creation, the pursuit of wisdom, through mystical elation or luminous calm.

'The greatest good,' wrote Spinoza, 'is the knowledge of the union which the mind has with the whole nature', and those who have found this out, who have opened Nature's Dictionary of Synonyms, do not wish for any other. But we live in a civilization in which so few can experience it, where 'Le vrai, c'est le secret de quelques-uns', where those who have been fortunate are like competitors in a treasure hunt who, while the others are still elbowing each other about and knocking things over, in silence discover the clue, know that they are right and sit down.

Moreover, even as obscure poisons, foci of infection, septic teeth and germ-crowded colons play a part in the origins of insanity, so do slums, great cities, proletarian poverty and bourgeois boredom or tyrannies of family and herd contribute to obscure our sense of union with the physical world. 'The misery of mankind is manifold' and breeds everywhere the despair, fear, hate and destruction which ulcerate our peace. Nature is banished from our civilization, the seasons lose their rhythm, the fruits of the earth their savour, the animals, co-heirs of our planet, are wantonly exterminated, the God within us is denied and the God without. Wisdom and serenity become treasures to be concealed and happiness a lost art. Resentment triumphs; the frustrated 'Have-nots' massacre the 'Haves'. We are in fact within sight of achieving a world neurosis, a world in which atrophy of the instincts (except that of herd-slaughter), abuse of the intellect and perversion of the heart will obliterate our knowledge of the purpose of life: humanity will choke in its own bile.

When the present slaughter terminates humanity can survive only through a return to the idea of happiness as the highest good, happiness which lies not in Power or in the exercise of the Will, but in the flowering of the spirit, and which in an unwarped society should coincide with consciousness. The justification for the State therefore will consist in rendering the individuals who compose it happier than they can make themselves by helping them to fulfil their potentialities, to control their Promethean environment and to revere the Zeus-environment which they cannot master. When once we have discovered how pain and suffering diminish the personality and how joy alone increases it, then the morbid attraction which is felt for evil, pain and abnormality will have lost its power. Why do we reward our men of genius, our suicides, our madmen and the generally maladjusted with the melancholy honours of a posthumous curiosity? Because we know that it is our society which has condemned these men to death and which is guilty because, out of its own ignorance and malformation, it has persecuted those who were potential saviours; smiters of the rock who might have touched the spring of healing and brought us back into harmony with ourselves.

Somehow, then, and without going mad, we must learn from these madmen to reconcile fanaticism with serenity. Either one, taken alone, is disastrous, yet except through the integration of these two opposites there can be no great art and no profound happiness—and what else is worth having? For nothing can be accomplished without fanaticism and without serenity nothing can be enjoyed. Perfection of form or increase of knowledge, pursuit of fame or service to the community, love of God or god of Love,—we must select the Illusion which appeals to our temperament and embrace it with passion, if we want to be happy. This is the farewell autumn precept with which Palinurus takes leave of his fast-fading nightmare. ' J'ai cueilli ce brin de bruyère.'

And now one more year of knowing nothing has gone by: once more the Pleiads are sinking; the plane-tree is bare; the bowstring relaxed. Exorcized is the dark face from the island poplars, drowned in the swirl of the moon-tarnished river; dishonoured are the graves of the lemurs; untended the sepulchre of the Prince on Gavrinis, forgotten as an Andalusian dog.

But thou, mimosa-shaded Siagne, flowing clear between the two Saint-Cassiens, receive Palinurus,—gently bear him under the scented Tanneron, past Auribeau and Mandelieu and the shrine on the tufted mount of Venus to his tomb by the shore.[1]

There, in the harsh sunshine, among the sea-holly and the midday plant, eringo and mesembrianthemum, where the tide prints its colophon of burnt drift-wood and the last susurrus of the wave expires on the sand,— naked under his watery sign shall he come to rest; a man too trustful in the calm of sky and sea.

> 'O nimium coelo et pelago confise sereno
> Nudus in ignota, Palinure, jacebis harena.'

[1] Palinurus enters the Siagne by the deserted village of Saint-Cassien des Bois; from there he floats some ten miles down to the wooded mound of Arluc, where stands the chapel of Saint-Cassien, scene of a pilgrimage and other nocturnal festivities on July 23rd. The chapel, which is surrounded by ancient elms and cypresses, overlooks the old delta of the Siagne from the site of a pagan temple dedicated by Roman sailors to Venus. 'Nazarius, vir stenuus et pius, non ferens animas hominum illudi fraude diabolica, delubrum et aram impudicae Veneri prope pontem fluminis nunc vulgo nuncupati *Siagnia*, omnino eliminare curavit . . .'—(*Chronol. Lerin.*, II, p. 80.)
(The pious and energetic Nazarius would not permit men's minds to be deceived by a fraud of the Devil, and so he caused the ruined altar, dedicated to licentious Venus, to be utterly destroyed; that 'altar of the grove' on the mound called Arluc, by the bridge over the river now commonly known as the Siagne.)

Palinurus thus completes his periplus among the stone-pines on the beach by La Napoule. This is at variance with Virgil's account in which Æneas names after him Capo Palinuro on the Gulf of Policastro, and marks one more of the discrepancies which lead one to question the author's veracity.

WHO WAS PALINURUS?

'The winding shelves do us detain,
Till God, the Palinure returns again.'

FULLER, 1640: Joseph's Coat.

Let us examine him: study the Psychiatrist's confidential report.

REPORT

Diagnosis. Strongly marked palinuroid tendencies.

Prognosis. Grave.

Clinical Picture. The story of Palinurus is only to be found in the third, fifth and sixth books of Virgil's *Aeneid*. The third book forms part of Æneas' relation to Dido of the events that befell him after the fall of Troy and consequently everything and everyone in it are seen through his eyes. This may be a cause of subjective bias, where the references in that book are concerned.

Nothing is known of Palinurus' heredity except that, like the physician Iapyx, he was a Trojan and descended from Iasus. Æneas addresses him as 'Iaside Palinure'. There is no evidence of any inherited psychopathic tendency. The first mention of Palinurus exhibits him in a confusion-state and suggests that, although usually a well-adjusted and efficient member of society, the pilot was experiencing a temporary 'black-out'. The passage introduces that undulant sea-music which will accompany Palinurus on his all too rare appearances. The translator is Dryden.

> Now from the sight of Land our Gallies move,
> With only Seas around, and Skies above.
> When o'er our Heads, descends a burst of Rain;
> And Night, with sable Clouds involves the Main:
> The ruffling Winds the foamy Billows raise:
> The scatter'd Fleet is forc'd to sev'ral Ways:
> The face of Heav'n is ravish'd from our Eyes,
> And in redoubl'd Peals the roaring Thunder flies.
> Cast from our Course, we wander in the Dark;
> No Stars to guide, no point of Land to mark.
> Ev'n *Palinurus* no distinction found
> Betwixt the Night and Day; such Darkness reign'd
>   around.

('Palinurus in unda'—Note the theme at his first appearance.)

The storm casts the ships on the Strophades, where the Harpies foul and plunder the heroes' open-air buffet. In vain the trumpeter Misenus blows the call to action: the Harpies are attacked but prove invulnerable and one, Celæno, curses the leader and his band, prophesying war and famine. They set sail again, the dactylic sea music reappears—and with it the master pilot.

> 'Tendunt vela Noti; fugimus spumantibus undis.
> qua cursum ventusque gubernatorque vocabat.
> jam medio apparet fluctu nemorosa Zacynthos
> Dulichiumque Sameque et Neritos ardua saxis.'

'South winds stretch the sails, we run over the bubbling waters where the breezes and the Pilot call the course, now Zacynthos covered with woods appears in the middle of the sea, and Dulichium and Same and Neritus with its steep cliffs'—('Zante, Zante fiore di Levante'). . . .

At length the pilot's moment approaches—

> The Night proceeding on with silent pace,
> Stood in her noon; and view'd with equal Face
> Her steepy rise, and her declining Race,
> Then wakeful *Palinurus* rose, to spie
> The face of Heav'n, and the Nocturnal Skie;
> And listen'd ev'ry breath of Air to try:
> Observes the Stars, and notes their sliding Course:
> The *Pleiads*, *Hyads*, and their wat'ry force;
> And both the Bears is careful to behold;
> And bright *Orion* arm'd with burnish'd Gold.
> Then when he saw no threat'ning Tempest nigh,
> But a sure promise of a settled skie;
> He gave the Sign to weigh: we break our sleep;
> Forsake the pleasing Shore, and plow the Deep.

A situation of considerable strain arises on the passage between Scylla and Charybdis:

> First *Palinurus* to the Larboard veer'd;
> Then all the Fleet by his Example steer'd.
> To Heav'n aloft on ridgy Waves we ride;
> Then down to Hell descend, when they divide.
> And thrice our Gallies knock'd the stony ground,
> And thrice the hollow Rocks return'd the sound,
> And thrice we saw the Stars, that stood with dews
>   around.

Harpies, Scylla, Charybdis, the Cyclops, Etna in eruption! Each one of the trials which the exiled pilot must

128

have undergone could occasion an anxiety-neurosis or effort-syndrome in a man less well-balanced. One wonders how he reacted to Æneas' public account of them. Dido, we know, fell disastrously 'in love' with Æneas, and it is when he departs (Æneas abandoning her after their cave-wedding), that Palinurus speaks again. The fleet has stolen out in the early morning and Dido has set alight her funeral pyre whose glow the sailors see, but Æneas alone interprets rightly. At once a storm gets up.

> But soon the Heav'ns with shadows were o'erspread;
> A swelling Cloud hung hov'ring o'er their Head:
> Livid it look'd (the threat'ning of a Storm),
> Then Night and Horror Ocean's Face deform.
> The Pilot *Palinurus* cry'd aloud,
> 'What Gusts of Weather from that gath'ring Cloud
> My Thoughts presage; e'er yet the Tempest roars.
> Stand to your Tackle, Mates, and stretch your Oars;
> Contract your swelling Sails, and luff to Wind'
> The frighted Crew perform the Task assign'd,
> Then, to his fearless Chief, 'Not Heav'n,' said he,
> 'Tho' *Jove* himself shou'd promise *Italy*,
> Can stem the Torrent of this raging Sea.
> Mark how the shifting Winds from West arise,
> And what collected Night involves the Skies!
> Nor can our shaken Vessels live at Sea,
> Much less against the Tempest force their way;
> 'Tis fate diverts our Course; and Fate we must obey.
> Not far from hence, if I observ'd aright
> The southing of the Stars and Polar Light,
> *Sicilia* lies; whose hospitable Shores
> In safety we may reach with strugling oars' . . .
> The Course resolv'd, before the Western Wind
> They scud amain; and make the Port assign'd.

It seems clear that Palinurus who had led the fleet
between Scylla and Charybdis, recognized that this
storm could not be ridden out because he knew it
followed on Æneas' betrayal of Dido. He also read the
true meaning of the fire which they had seen and from
that moment realized that Æneas was guilty of hubris
and impiety; he was 'not the Messiah'.

In Sicily Æneas celebrates his arrival with elaborate
games. In these—although they include various sailing
contests—Palinurus himself does not join and lets the
other pilots fight them out. One can imagine him brood-
ing over the storm and his leader's conduct while the
noisy sport proceeds around him. Finally, to prevent the
men leaving, the women set fire to the ships and four are
destroyed. Here occurs an incident for which no scientific
explanation is forthcoming, and which, if the narrator
were Palinurus and not Virgil, we would be tempted to
ascribe to a delusion of reference. Venus begs Neptune
to guarantee that her beloved Æneas and all his men will
not be subjected to any more disasters and storms at sea
by their enemy, Juno. Neptune agrees, but warns her
that 'In safety as thou prayest shall he reach the haven of
Avernus. Only one shall there be whom, lost in the flood,
thou shalt seek in vain; one life shall be given for many.'

> 'Unus erit tantum, amissum quem gurgite quaeres
> unum pro multis dabitur caput.'

Then the fleet sets sail.

> A Head of all the Master Pilot steers
> And as he leads, the following Navy veers.
> The Steeds of Night had travell'd half the Sky,
> The drowsy Rowers on their Benches lye;
> When the soft God of Sleep, with easie flight,
> Descends, and draws behind a trail of Light.

WHO WAS PALINURUS?

Thou *Palinurus* art his destin'd Prey;
To thee alone he takes his fatal way.
Dire Dreams to thee, and Iron Sleep he bears;
And lighting on thy Prow, the Form of *Phorbas*
    wears.
Then thus the Traitor God began his Tale:
'The Winds, my Friend, inspire a pleasing gale;
The Ships, without thy Care, securely sail.
Now steal an hour of sweet Repose; and I
Will take the Rudder, and thy room supply.'
To whom the yauning Pilot, half asleep;
'Me dost thou bid to trust the treach'rous Deep!
The Harlot-smiles of her dissembling Face,
And to her Faith commit the *Trojan* Race?
Shall I believe the *Syren* South again,
And, oft betray'd, not know the Monster Main?'
He said, his fasten'd hands the Rudder keep,
And fix'd on Heav'n, his Eyes repel invading Sleep.
The God was wroth, and at his Temples threw
A Branch in *Lethe* dip'd, and drunk with *Stygian*
    Dew:
The Pilot, vanquish'd by the Pow'r Divine,
Soon clos'd his swimming Eyes, and lay supine.
Scarce were his Limbs extended at their length,
The God, insulting with superior Strength,
Fell heavy on him, plung'd him in the Sea,
And, with the Stern, the Rudder tore away.
Headlong he fell, and struggling in the Main,
Cry'd out for helping hands, but cry'd in vain:
The Victor Dæmon mounts obscure in Air;
While the Ship sails without the Pilot's care.
On *Neptune's* Faith the floating Fleet relies;
But what the Man forsook, the God supplies;
And o'er the dang'rous Deep secure the Navy flies.
Glides by the *Syren's* Cliffs, a shelfy Coast,
Long infamous for Ships, and Sailors lost;

And white with Bones: Th' impetuous Ocean
    roars;
And Rocks rebellow from the sounding Shores.
The watchful Heroe felt the knocks; and found
The tossing Vessel sail'd on shoaly Ground.
Sure of his Pilot's loss, he takes himself
The Helm, and steers aloof, and shuns the Shelf.
Inly he griev'd; and groaning from the Breast,
Deplor'd his Death; and thus his Pain express'd:
'For Faith repos'd on Seas, and on the flatt'ring
    Sky,
Thy naked Corps is doom'd, on Shores unknown to
    lye.'

The account is full of difficulties. 'Te Palinure petens, tibi somnia tristia portans insonti'—'Looking for *you*, Palinurus, bringing you sad visions, guiltless though you are.' But was Palinurus guiltless? If, as we suggest, he was tired of the fruitless voyage, horrified by the callousness of Æneas, by the disasters which he seemed to attract by his rowdy games, by the ultimate burning of some of the ships by the angry women,—that act unforgivable in the eyes of a man of the sea,—then was his disappearance as accidental as Æneas supposed? Sleep first appears disguised as Phorbas. Now Phorbas was already dead— killed in the siege of Troy. He represents the 'old school' of Trojan. In Virgil's account, the God of Sleep is angry when Palinurus refuses the first temptation. But surely the clue we should notice is that, although the sea is calm, Palinurus when he falls takes with him tiller, rudder and a section of poop. Tillers may come off easily but not part of the stern! Thus he provides himself not only with a raft but inflicts a kind of castration on Æneas by removing both his chief pilot and his means of steering, and this within the dangerous orbit of the Sirens! Surely this is a typical example of anti-social hysteroid resentment! And how does Æneas take the helm, when it is there no longer?[1]

Æneas' last words 'For Faith repos'd on seas . . .':

> 'O nimium coelo et pelago confise sereno
> nudus in ignota, Palinure, jacebis harena.'

are doubly ironical—for Palinurus boasted that he was far too experienced to trust the sea again ('Mene huic confidere monstro?'), and Dido has also prayed for exactly the same fate for Æneas,—'Let him fall before his time'—'Sed cadat ante diem mediaque inhumatus harena', 'and lie unburied amid the sand'. It would not be fair to the reader to let this subject pass without referring to Mr. W. F. Jackson Knight's fascinating study, *Cumæan Gates* (Basil Blackwell), where he makes the supposition that Palinurus' removal of the stern of the ship was a Virgilian echo of the Babylonian Epic of Gilgamish, in which Gilgamish, bound for the lower regions, loses some essential part of his boat, and has to cut himself a quantity of punt-poles, even as Æneas had to lop the Golden Bough, to ensure his crossing to the underworld.

Palinurus, still clutching the tiller of his improvized raft, tosses on the pallid wastes of the heaving Sicilian. Three times the red sun sinks and the sheen of opal darkens on the cold and ancient gristle of the sea, three times the cloudswept Pleiads glimmer from the rainy South before at last the creaming and insouciant surf relinquishes its prey. On the Lucanian shore by Velia he lands and is immediately set upon by the brutish inhabitants. Not having received burial, he must wait a hundred years on the banks of the Styx before he can

---

[1] 'What the Man forsook, the God supplies' is an interpolation of Dryden's. Clavus (key, tiller) can also mean penis.

cross. Here Æneas, on his official visit to the Shades,
rejoins him, to whom Palinurus at once appeals, pro-
testing his innocence in a manner with which those who
have had experience of such patients are familiar.

> Amidst the Spirits *Palinurus* press'd;
> Yet fresh from life; a new admitted Guest.
> Who, while he steering view'd the Stars, and bore
> His Course from *Affrick*, to the *Latian* Shore,
> Fell headlong down. The *Trojan* fix'd his view,
> And scarcely through the gloom the sullen Shadow
>   knew.
> Then thus the Prince. 'What envious Pow'r, O
>   Friend,
> Brought your lov'd Life to this disastrous end?
> For *Phœbus*, ever true in all he said,
> Has, in your fate alone, my Faith betray'd?
> To God foretold you shou'd not die, before
> You reach'd, secure from Seas, th' *Italian* Shore?
> Is this th' unerring Pow'r?' The Ghost reply'd,
> 'Nor *Phœbus* flatter'd, nor his Answers ly'd;
> Nor envious Gods have sent me to the Deep:
> But while the Stars, and course of Heav'n I keep,
> My weary'd Eyes were seiz'd with fatal sleep.[1]
> I fell; and with my weight, the Helm constrain'd,
> Was drawn along, which yet my gripe retain'd.
> Now by the Winds, and raging Waves, I swear,
> Your Safety, more than mine, was then my Care:
> Lest, of the Guide bereft, the Rudder lost,
> Your Ship shou'd run against the rocky Coast.
> Three blust'ring Nights, born by the Southern blast,
> I floated; and discover'd Land at last:

[1] In the original, Palinurus makes no mention of being
asleep, nor is there any other mention of Apollo's prophecy,
which may be a trap set by Æneas. Notice how Palinurus'
reply is calculated to allay suspicion.

High on a mounting Wave, my head I bore:
Forcing my Strength, and gath'ring to the Shore:
Panting, but past the danger, now I seiz'd
The Craggy Cliffs, and my tir'd Members eas'd:
While, cumber'd with my dropping Cloaths, I lay,
The cruel Nation, covetous of Prey,
Stain'd with my Blood th' unhospitable Coast:
And now, by Winds and Waves, my lifeless Limbs
    are tost.
Which, O avert, by yon Ethereal Light
Which I have lost, for this eternal Night:
Or, if by dearer ties you may be won,
By your dead Sire, and by your living Son,
Redeem from this Reproach, my wand'ring Ghost;
Or with your Navy seek the *Velin* Coast:
And in a peaceful Grave my Corps compose:
Or, if a nearer way your Mother shows,
Without whose Aid, you durst not undertake
This frightful Passage o'er the *Stygian* Lake;
Lend to this Wretch your Hand, and waft him o'er
To the sweet Banks of yon forbidden Shore.'
Scarce had he said, the Prophetess began;
'What hopes delude thee, miserable Man?
Think'st thou thus unentomb'd to cross the Floods,
To view the Furies, and Infernal Gods;
And visit, without leave, the dark abodes?
Attend the term of long revolving years:
Fate, and the dooming Gods, are deaf to Tears.
This Comfort of thy dire Misfortune take;
The Wrath of Heav'n, inflicted for thy sake,
With Vengeance shall pursue th' inhuman Coast.
Till they propitiate thy offended Ghost,
And raise a Tomb, with Vows, and solemn Pray'r;
And *Palinurus*' name the Place shall bear.'
This calm'd his Cares: sooth'd with his future Fame;
And pleas'd to hear his propagated Name.

It is noteworthy that not Æneas, but the stern Sibyl makes reply. Palinurus moreover makes no mention of having fallen asleep, but says 'the helm was violently torn from him'. It is worth remarking that his fate bears a close resemblance to that of Elpenor, in the Eleventh Odyssey. We may contrast Palinurus' appeal 'nunc me fluctus habet . . . da dextram misero' with Elpenor's request for a burial and a proper tombstone, 'memorial of an unhappy man for those who come after'.

His death is very closely paralleled by that of Misenus, the trumpeter of Æneas, who was drowned in the surf at Cumae a few days after Palinurus, while Æneas was consulting the Sibyl and whose fame was also secured after burial by the naming of a cape after him. Misenus may never have recovered from the ignominy of his ineffectual trumpeting to the Harpies. That Æneas should lose two of his most skilled technicians, pilot and trumpeter, and shortly afterwards, his old nurse, Caieta, at this moment when he visits the underworld, and there consecrates himself entirely to his Empire-building mission, may suggest that there was an 'old guard' who had had enough of him, who unconsciously did not wish to enter the promised land or to go through with the slaughter necessary to possess it.[1]

Phrontis, pilot of Menelaus, also died mysteriously while at the helm off Cape Sunium (Od. iii, l. 285).

---

[1] 'Virgil knew the cost of Empire; the cost in suffering, and the cost to conscience and to so many graceful things. That he knew the cost his poem shows so clearly that it has lately been thought to be a savage attack on Augustus and autocracy'.— W. J. KNIGHT, op. cit. p. 168.

The Palinurus passages are so charged with haunting images and golden cadences as to suggest that Virgil has identified himself with his pilot (as did Milton with Orpheus). Both poets reflect their unconscious death-wish. Palinurus: Æneas:: Virgil: Augustus.

WHO WAS PALINURUS?

Virgil in fact makes use of three doubles: Palinurus–
Phrontis, the pilot who falls into the sea, Palinurus–
Elpenor, the unburied corpse who pleads with the hero
in hell, and Palinurus–Misenus, the Cape-christener.
Dionysus records an older tradition in which Æneas and
his fleet first touched land at Cape Palinuro, in which
case Virgil has stolen the honour from the pilot for Cape
Miseno and Cumæ.

Those are all the known facts about Palinurus.
Whether he deliberately tried to abandon Æneas,
whether he was the innocent victim of divine vengeance
or a melancholy and resentful character who felt his
special nautical gift was soon to become unwanted cannot
be deduced from the evidence. His bluff sailor's manner
may belie his real state of mind. I am inclined to rule out
both suicide (there are no symptoms comparable to those
of Dido when she felt all nature prompting her to the
deed) and accident, for the sterns of ships do not fall off
in calm seas. We are left, therefore, with design—a
planned act of escape and revenge by Palinurus—or with
supernatural intervention, in the shape of a propitiatory
sacrifice of the Pilot to Juno, who might otherwise have
prevented the safe arrival of Æneas and his whole
expedition.

Which of these alternatives we accept is, in the last
analysis, a question of the claims of reason versus those
of revealed religion.

As a myth, however, and particularly as a myth with
a valuable psychological interpretation, Palinurus clearly
stands for a certain will-to-failure or repugnance-to-
success, a desire to give up at the last moment, an urge
towards loneliness, isolation and obscurity. Palinurus, in
spite of his great ability and his conspicuous public
position, deserted his post in the moment of victory and
opted for the unknown shore.

With the sea—age-old symbol of the unconscious—his relations were always close and harmonious, and not until he reaches land is he miserably done to death.

And as with so many of those who resign from the struggle, who quit because they do not want to succeed, because they find something vulgar and even unlucky in success itself—immediately he feels remorse and misery at his abdication and wishes he had stuck to his job. Doing is overrated and success undesirable, but even more so the bitterness of Failure. Palinurus, in fact, though he despises the emptiness of achievement, the applause of the multitude and the rewards of fame, comes in his long exile to hate himself for this contempt and so he jumps childishly at the chance to be perpetuated as an obscure cape.[1]

One last clue: The name Palinurus (παλίνουρος) in Greek, (and we know the importance attached to their names by neurotics), means 'one-who-makes-water-again', and is so used in an epigram of Martial (III. 78)—

> 'Minxisti currente semel, Pauline, carina.
> Meiere vis iterum? Jam Palinurus eris.'

'You have made water once, Paulinus, while your boat was moving fast. Do you want to pumpship again? Then you will Palinurinate' (i.e. will fall overboard).

These words 'ουρεῖν, mingere, meiere, possess as well a sexual significance and this opens up possibilities of a deep analysis on Freudian lines, should time permit —and funds be available.

---

[1] Cape Palinuro soon acquired a reputation for shipwrecks. The Roman Fleet met with disaster there in 253 B.C., and again in 36 B.C. Horace also had a narrow escape. On the summit of the headland (home of *primula Palinuri*) are visible some ruins which are popularly known as the Tomb of Palinurus. The promontory, through which runs Lat. 40°, retains its ancient name.

INDEX

INDEX

INDEX